PRAISE

"With deepest gratitude, I sit—quietly sobbing, for Divinely guided I have been to the words Elizabeth has so carefully tended. Her inspiration is and will be the catalyst for healing. *The Light Within* surfaced many emotions that I had buried, religiously. Finally, perhaps, they are ready to be untethered and set free. The honest portrayal of her traumatic situations and her triumph will help set us all free!"

—SHARON CASSANOLOCHMAN, award-winning, #1 international bestselling author of several books, including *Stranded on Thin Ice* (www.sharoncassanolochman.com), and book coach

"Elizabeth truly has provided a gift to me and her readers. I love how she has woven everything together—journal entries, family background, and exploration of her inner landscape. She establishes personal rapport with her readers by confiding in them as if a close friend and also allowing them their space. Truly a gift."

—REV. DR. DEBBIE MOODY, MHS/PHC

"Elizabeth Onyeabor's writing is captivating and inspirational. *The Light Within* reveals how, through self-love and compassion, we can tap into our creative gifts that have remained dormant due to our own self-induced guilt to heal our soul and mind. This book gives you the powerful tools to help you heal and move forward to live a life with more freedom and joy."

—GENA ANDERSON, CPC, SPHR, ELI-MP, Leadership and Career Development Coach

"You can't give what you don't have. In her most recent work, *The Light Within*, Elizabeth Onyeabor shares openly, and lovingly, all that her soul bears, and then some. Her poetic writing is infused with wisdom, gained only from a deep dive of processing, integrating, and accepting her human experience on Earth. Elizabeth shares how she processed her experiences, giving a glimpse of just a sliver of her incredible courage and strength. This story can only be told from one who has walked with her shadow. It is only when we can embrace our pain, integrate our experiences, thank it and release it for how it has served us, that we can then embrace the wholeness of our being. Her gentle guidance creates sacred space for anyone on a healing journey, returning the reader to the love and the light within, found in every sacred heart."

—EVELYN FOREMAN, author,
Attract the Love of Your Life (www.evelynforeman.com)

"Every parent knows the pain of feeling like they're failing their kids--even when they're not. In her newest book, *The Light Within*, Elizabeth Onyeabor shares her journey through decades of guilt and shame to finally make peace with her parenting choices and heal herself. In this raw and vulnerable memoir, Onyeabor explores unconventional ways to release the shame and guilt—it goes beyond 'knowing' and brings the reader access to a powerful feeling that all is well. It's part nurturing safe place and part road map for all who have their own wounds to heal—a must-read for parents who have trouble forgiving themselves and seeing that their best isn't just good enough, but exactly what their families need."

—ERICA RODEFER WINTERS,
Founder, Spoiled Yogi (www.spoiledyogi.com)

THE LIGHT WITHIN

OTHER BOOKS BY ELIZABETH

From the Shadows: A Journey of Self-Discovery and Renewal
(Sojourn Publishing)

Escaping the Shadows: A Pilgrimage with Poetry
(Achara Bambus Creative Works)

Elizabeth Onyeabor books are available for order through Amazon.com and other retailers.

My Gift to You

Deepen your experience with
The Light Within: Practice Guide and visualization recordings.

*3 Keys to Feel Good Enough:
A 30-Day Guide for a More Joyful You*
(Achara Bambus Creative Works)
Free ebook

Available only at www.ElizabethOnyeabor.com/gifts

THE LIGHT WITHIN

Freedom Through Forgiveness

Elizabeth Onyeabor

The Light Within: Freedom Through Forgiveness
Copyright © 2021 Elizabeth Onyeabor
Achara Bambus Creative Works, LLC
All rights reserved.

Selections from *Mary DeLaMare Pederson: Excerpts from her Diaries and Letters 1933-1980* (unpublished manuscript) copyright © 2004 Kathleen Pederson Whitworth and selections from *From the Shadows: A Journey of Self-Discovery and Renewal* copyright © 2016 Elizabeth Onyeabor, reprinted with permission.

No part of this book may be reproduced, stored in a retrieval system, or transmitted, in any form or by any means—electronic, mechanical, photocopying, recording, or otherwise—without the author's prior written permission. The only exception is by a reviewer who may quote short excerpts in a review with proper citations.

Book cover design by Debbie O'Byrne (www.jetlaunch.net) and Elizabeth Onyeabor
Editing by Eye Comb Editors (www.eyecombeditors.com) and Tracy Black of Tracy Black Consulting
Visit my website for gifts
Website: elizabethonyeabor.com/gifts

Connect with me on social media.
LinkedIn: linkedin.com/in/elizabethonyeabor
Twitter: twitter.com/efonyeabor
Instagram: instagram.com/elizabethonyeabor
Facebook: facebook.com/elizabethonyeaborauthor

First Printing: July 2021.
Publisher: Achara Bambus Creative Works, LLC
ISBN-13: 978-1-955681001 (paperback)
ISBN 13: 978-1-955681018 (digital)

Printed in the United States of America.

Disclaimer: The contents of this book ("Content") are for informational purposes only; the Content is not intended to be a substitute for professional medical advice, diagnosis, or treatment. Always seek the guidance of your doctor or other qualified health professional with questions you may have regarding your health or a medical condition. Never disregard the advice of a medical professional or delay in seeking it because of something you read in this book. If you rely on any information provided in *The Light Within*, you do so solely at your own risk. Under no circumstances is the author or Achara Bambus Creative Works, LLC responsible for the claims of third-party websites or educational providers.

DEDICATION

For the "Frances" in all of us

The wound is the place where the light enters you.

—Rumi

ACKNOWLEDGMENTS

Thanks to my family. They made this book possible by telling their stories and providing support and encouragement.

My darling husband Gillis Onyeabor's unwavering support and encouragement helped me hole up in my writing room for hours on end while I connected with the past. A motherhood forgiveness account can't be complete without thanking those who made me a mom. I appreciate Victoria Onyeabor, Kenneth Onyeabor, and Christopher Onyeabor for everything they've taught me about love.

My siblings are a blessing. My bond with Kathleen Whitworth, Kristine Giles, Yvonne Krause, Steven Pederson, and Quintin Pederson deepens through profound discoveries. Thanks for our discussions and sharing your perspectives of events.

I appreciate each family member for cheering me on even though by sharing my stories, I reveal parts of theirs from my unique perspective.

Fortunately, many ancestors kept and compiled journals or otherwise recorded histories. Special thanks go to Kathleen, who spent countless hours collecting and documenting Mom's history and allowed me to reprint portions from her collection. Kathleen compiled the most extensive set of memories and documentation about Grandpa Rob and his family. She also made sure I had copies of other histories assembled by our cousins.

In addition to my recollections and correspondence, I

checked documents written by my ancestors for verifying facts. The references section includes a full listing.

Feedback early on from my author group friends Ernestine Colombo, Sharon CassanoLochman, Debbie Moody, Frank Elliott, and Evelyn Foreman proved invaluable. Special thanks go to Ernestine and Sharon for their second reads and helpful feedback. Despite the rough shape of my manuscript, they still encouraged me to share my stories.

Tori Yabo and her team at Eye Comb Editors provided unique insights and took my messages to a deeper and clearer level. As a second set of eyes, Tracy Black of Tracy Black Consulting suggested spot-on tweaks. I'm not sure how Debbie O'Byrne at JetLaunch does it, but she followed my vague ideas and designed the ideal cover. I appreciate everyone who supported me in the process of birthing this book.

CONTENTS

INTRODUCTION	1
TREATING THE TRAUMA	5
1 Cuddle Chair	7
2 Diving Deeper	9
3 Beth Beckons	21
4 Mother Mary	25
5 Nice Neighbor	31
SUPPRESSING EXPRESSION	35
6 What About Woody?	37
7 Sorrowful Surrender	49
8 Reluctant Remorse	55
9 Footsteps to Follow	61
10 Motherhood Malaise	67
PASSIONS AND POISONS	73
11 Johnny's Jewel	75
12 Persnickety Passion	77
13 Finding Frances	85
14 Tweeded Tormentor	89
15 My Mirrors	93
JUGGLING JUDGMENTS	101
16 Compassionate Compositions	103
17 Facing Fear	107
18 Flowing Formations	113
19 Dance Among Daisies	117
20 Parental Propagandizer	121
PICKING PERSPECTIVES	129
21 Radiant Resurrection	131

22 Love's Light	135
23 Challenging Choices	139
24 Ancestral Appreciation	143
25 Inner Inspiration	147
26 Drama's Détente	151
27 Outlook Opting	157
FREEDOM THROUGH FORGIVENESS	**163**
28 Vicarious Vindication	165
29 Final Forgiveness	169
30 Elizabeth's Enough	173
31 Cleansing Compassion	181
32 Wholesome Homecoming	185
33 Shared Sphere	189
REFLECT AND RESPOND	**197**
Practice 1: Healing Her-story and His-story	199
Practice 2: Bearing Burdens	205
Practice 3: Aged Assurance	207
Practice 4: Forging Through Five	209
Practice 5: Caged Conditioning	211
Practice 6: Deltoid Dialog	213
Practice 7: Comforting Caress	217
Practice 8: Soothing Self-Compassion	219
Practice 9: Propagandizing Prattle	221
Practice 10: Blossoming Brilliance	223
Practice 11: Inner Insights	225
Practice 12: Finding Your Frances	227
REFERENCES	**231**
ABOUT THE AUTHOR	**233**

INTRODUCTION

TAKE A DEEP dive into how I healed from the stubborn remnants of what caused my worst depression: mom guilt and shame powered by the need to make things perfect. As I was completing *From the Shadows,* about my descent into and journey out of despair, I started this book in parallel. I knew I had to forgive myself.

Plus, I was struggling with a whole new set of triggers. I dug up a traumatic memory from childhood involving a man who lived nearby. Although forty-eight years had passed, the heaviness of the memory crushed me as much as that day when I was six. I wanted to finally heal. I needed a way to let go of the pain.

In this book, I invite you into my mind. I show you how I forgave myself, dealt with my neighbor, and reclaimed innocence and self-love.

Soul-searching led me to talk with my mom, grandma, and an aunt. Their stories stirred me. I followed their guidance and wrote what I heard to create this book's first draft. Then, I shelved my manuscript.

Their encouragement had worked, but I still had to overcome my discomfort with releasing this book. After almost a year's hiatus, I began editing and writing these stories again.

But two issues worried me. First, I wrestled with transparency versus privacy and balanced portrayals about my loved ones. I discussed my descriptions and fact-checked certain sections with my family.

Second, I grappled with how to describe my conversations with Mom, Grandma, and Great-Grandaunt Frances. I was too embarrassed to share outside my inner circle. Were they in heaven talking to me? Was I channeling them? Would I sound nutso? Was it all in my head? I wasn't sure what to think. It took two more years to sort out my understanding and what I would share with others.

What I accepted from the start was the marvelous sensation flowing through me when I brought them to mind. Time and time again, I drew from their inspiration as a wellspring of healing and forgiveness. Now, I couldn't envision better companions for this journey.

Through written accounts and their personal histories, I did my best to validate what I heard Mom, Grandma, and Aunt Frances say. No doubt, I filtered what they told me through my own terms and experiences. Some aspects of their lives weren't documented, so I couldn't authenticate everything we discussed. However, each detail, conversation, and story they shared played a genuine part in my healing process.

I condensed and clarified Mom's journal entries and history excerpts; otherwise, they're unedited. As creative as she was, I doubt she could've imagined her notes back then would uplift me so many decades later.

Some events and details I kept private, although I described how I approached them. Sure, I took a few artistic liberties. Mostly, I changed some names and other details to maintain privacy, preserve anonymity, or avoid confusion.

I shouted swear words when strong emotions carried me away. Thanks in advance for your understanding.

After my stories, I posed questions for your response and reflection. They're the same guideposts I followed in my healing. Use them to find your freedom through forgiveness.

TREATING THE TRAUMA

*You need to acknowledge the anger
before you can release it*

1 CUDDLE CHAIR

Mary Poppins, practically perfect . . .

BUNCHES OF MAUVE and lavender lilacs hang from silvery green boughs, all papering the wall behind the chestnut-gold love seat. She sits on its circular cushion resting against its comfy back. Brunette bangs brush against her forehead. The rest of her hair sweeps back to her nape while her ears play peek-a-boo through the hairspray's hold. Her sparkling eyes match her sky-blue blouse and complement her white skirt suit.

I snuggle and nestle my head on her bosom. Our chests rise and fall in tune with our hearts' warm waltz while my lungs tango with her musky Tabu perfume. The woven seat embraces a five- or six-foot width. Our legs sprawl in front of us, and our size-ten bare feet dangle several inches over its edge. I call it the cuddle chair.

We share similar oval-shaped faces, except my hairline curves into a widow's peak. Her complexion flows creamy buttermilk while mine sprays faint freckles. Today, my eyes appear more green than blue, reflecting my emerald blouse. She twirls my wispy blonde tendrils around her forefinger. Her soprano timbre caresses me. "You're forgiven when you forgive yourself. You didn't fail as a mother. Your children love you. You called me 'Mary Poppins, practically perfect.' The 'practically perfect' part meant I wasn't flawless. You're not perfect, either, and never will be.

"You would've made different choices if you'd known. But you didn't. No need to obsess over your shortcomings anymore.

"Let the light within you shine. Allow its radiance to ignite others with an inspirational flame."

After tucking a wavy lock behind my ear, her fingertips trace a tender line along my cheek and chin. From where she ends, the sensation continues a soothing course on its own until supple energy fills my heart.

"Thanks for your unconditional love, Mom. I love you."

She fades from my imagination.

2 DIVING DEEPER

Masticates the memory . . .

SOON AFTER VISITING with Mom, I'm gliding through my day when I suspect it's time to dive into deeper waters and resurface another relic.

Until a year ago, despair sank me into fathomless peril during my darkest days. Through exploration, I emerged buoyant with newfound awareness and healing. No longer drowning, I swam in emotional self-care. Although I started with a forward crawl, I tried backstroke, butterfly, and breaststroke techniques until I found my freestyle.

My self-discovery voyage never ends.

I hold enormous love for Mom, but a sense of desertion lingers. My childish fantasy insists she could have protected me from *him*, if only she were a stay-at-home mother.

She's not the only one I blame.

I retreat to my writing room to reflect.

A king-sized guest bed, covered with a white-and-sea-green paisley cover, lounges along an inner wall while my writing space spans an outer wall opposite it.

As I settle into my black-mesh writing chair, I kick off my flip flops. My soles cool on the marbled tiles. The writing chair's lumbar cushion and headrest hold my back and neck in a ready-made hug. The white laminate desktop straddles two lateral file cabinets, allowing space to prop my feet on a stool below.

Artwork adorns the wall in front of me. Directly above my desk hangs a mauve, lavender, and green watercolor edged with a silvery frame. The landscape reminds me of the western USA, where I grew up. My two grandmothers hang out with me, in oil portrait reprints. To my left, Nana's black and gray-streaked hair forms a loose knot atop her head. From a Rembrandt-style backdrop, her tanned and wrinkled face holds quiet contemplation. To my right, Grandma Mary's chestnut-brown hair peeks out under a derby hat with a feather plume. Her porcelain face radiates a Monet's airiness from its pastel canvas.

Atop my desk, my laptop waits. I open a new document, type today's date at the top, and squish lavender-tipped earbuds into place. I roll my teal trackball to the "Christopher's Compilations" folder and right-click to randomize ten songs for as long as today's writing session lasts. My muscles soften as the techno vibes ripple through my core.

The silvery-framed watercolor holds my gaze while my fingers prepare to plunge from the *asdf* and *jkl;* keys.

I lean against the headrest, close my eyes, and take one deep breath in and out. Tingles cascade from my crown to my toes. I draw in a second. My third gradual inhale and exhale springboards me into inspiration.

With each keystroke, my fingers start another swim in scenes from my soul.

The watercolor's landscape blends into bunches of lilacs surrounding the cuddle chair.

I dip beyond its comfort and purposely plummet into an ocean of emotion about what I submerged at age six.

The Light Within

⋘⋙

Cheery orange faces and black noses dot the driveway's north side. I stroll past the poppies, toward my neighbor's charcoal-gray home. Sunshine highlights honey-colored strands throughout my brown, pixie-cut hair. Tan freckles sprinkle across my nose and cheeks. I plan to bake goodies with Mrs. Joren, my substitute grandmother. I relish spending time with her when I'm not playing with children or visiting other adults in my neighborhood.

A constant dill scent permeates her house, and clear jars display assorted fruit and vegetable preserves along her pantry shelves. Mrs. Joren dons her black dress, black stockings, and black shoes as she always has since her husband passed. Her silvery hair spirals in a low bun at the back of her neck. Her gingerbread brown eyes and crinkled face always brighten around me. After today's baking, she leaves me in the kitchen. Phil enters and greets me. He's one of two bachelor sons living with her. He mentions a surprise he wants to show me, but I need to head upstairs.

His forty-year-old legs carry him in quick strides along the treads. I saunter up the steps, trailing my hand along the dark wooden banister and its smooth sheen. I enjoy sliding my palm along the varnish.

Phil waits for me at the stairway's top, arms crossed, lips shut tight, clothed in a white shirt and black pants. His raven mustache matches his straight hair trimmed just above his collar and ears. He parts it on the side and keeps it slicked down with pomade. He taps his foot as if doing so will make me climb faster.

Phil ushers me into his bedroom. A walnut armoire covers half the wall to my left, and its matching four-poster bed lies to my right. I stand on a multi-colored rug and compare it with the rugs Nana braided at my home. When I hear the door shut, I turn around.

He closes in, opposite me, and glances behind his shoulder. "This is a special sharing time that we need to keep secret."

My head nods up and down. "I promise."

His brown eyes darken and narrow while his hushed tenor coaxes and cajoles. But what he's urging me to do unravels my comfort. I tune him out and focus on the Adam's apple bobbing in his neck.

Phil drops his pants to his ankles to reveal his underwear. He shows me "his" and wants me to show him "mine." A hidden knot in my chest tightens; its slack slips to my feet and lashes them in place. I stand immobile in my purple and white polka-dot dress and white, T-strap sandals.

He snarls something and takes control. As his puppet, he yanks invisible strings on my body. The braided rug cushions my head when it hits the floor. He hovers over me. His elbow holds me in place, stabbing the right side of my chest like a puppeteer's crossbar impaling my soul.

All my screams suffocate inside my head before they can make any sound, but he covers my mouth anyway. Silent tears stream along my temples and drown in my damp hair.

My legs and arms thicken into useless sticks of wood. I stare at Mr. and Mrs. Joren's photographs on the dresser, wishing she could rescue me. I refuse to keep looking at what Phil insists I should stroke.

Fortunately, Mrs. Joren calls for Phil, as if she heard my silent pleas. She's distracted him before he makes me touch that ugly thing or does something worse. I snap alert. When he hobbles to open the door and reply, I squeeze past him and dash down the stairs. I race out the front door, sprint home, and leave my white panties behind.

Scrunched on my bedroom floor, I pull my knees to my chest and cover my legs with my dress, all the way to my ankles. I interlock my arms around my knees and rock back and forth. My shrieks puncture my heaving breaths.

I hide in my closet, a new, safe-haven cave of my creation where I bury our secret. I'm so successful, I smother all my emotions—from suffering to passion.

Unwittingly, I also inter my creativity and childhood desire to be a writer.

⊂৪⊃

I hunch over my writing desk and rock back and forth while my face flushes, lips quiver, and eyes brim to overflow.

Tears pepper my cheeks, and my stomach churns. I explode in bawls so loud and long my throat burns.

Phil snatched this away from her.

Away from me.

A growing fury dries my tears. My ribcage grips my breath. A pain pierces my right side. My jaw clenches as if I'm chewing, but only masticates the memory.

Why that?

Why then?

Why him?

Why me?

The *whys* provoke so many unanswered questions about a past I can't change.

Until recently, I didn't allow myself to remember what

happened in Phil's room. The assault unearthed itself in a muddle while I wrote my *From the Shadows* manuscript several months ago.

As I wrote that book, I discovered how I had disconnected two parts of myself. My feelings side was stuck in my child self, Beth, an identity I thought I silenced as a teenager. It was an unconscious attempt to rid myself of the wounds she represented. Instead, Beth's suffering shadowed me as I adopted Liz, who was logical and distanced herself from emotions, until at fifty years old, Liz wanted to kill herself.

As I healed from depression over the last several years, I connected the heart of Beth with the head of Liz and became whole again as Elizabeth. Now, I'm moving forward on my healing journey but still reeling from this freshly surfaced trauma and the true extent of Beth's wounds.

Continuing with this burden in tow isn't healthy. I don't want Phil bogging me down anymore. Let me sail freely with my newfound writing passion.

How can I do that?

In my writing chair, I sit straight and take three gradual inhales and exhales, allowing my fingers to storm the scene.

I will confront Phil.

☙❧

Without focusing on his features, I bring to mind only his shadowy form. Ripping off the memory's pall compels me to shout.

"It all started with you, Phil Joren. You stole my innocence. You robbed my passion.

"Do you realize the torment you provoked for *forty-eight*

years? I blame you. You need to take accountability for your actions.

"Maybe you were, you were a pervert preying on a terrified little girl who couldn't say no. Maybe you didn't believe you had control or influence over anything else in your life.

"I don't know why you did what you did. Frankly, I don't even care.

"You're disgusting. You are a bastard! A fucking bastard!"

With my rage released, the vitriol pumping through my veins disperses, and exhaustion drains me.

I slip away from my writing chair, sink onto the guest bed, and surrender to slumber.

೦౩೮౦

Once I wake from my nap, I want to resume my earlier conversation with Mom. Again, I ease into my writing chair, take deep breaths, and allow my mind to relax in the cuddle chair's comfort.

Mom joins me, bare feet crossed. Her arms rest along the cushioned back while mine fold across my chest.

For the first time, I fill her in about what happened at the Joren house and how I'm trying to reconcile everything.

"I'm so angry about Phil. What a perv. Wish it never happened. I hate what he did to me."

I pause. I don't want to hold my other grudge any longer but see no way to soften it.

"And I hate that you weren't home."

Her eyes widen.

"Sorry," I say.

Mom wraps her arms around me. "Hon, I'm so sorry for everything. If I could have . . . had I known . . ."

Shudders run down Mom's spine before she shakes them off.

"Had I known, if I had any idea then, we would've done something."

She pats my thigh.

"I'm so proud of you. Boy, what a brave escape. But all these years, keeping such a secret. Oh, sweetie."

I sob into her sleeve, and she rubs my back.

"You need to acknowledge the anger before you can release it, anyway."

Each sniffle tugs on inner resolve.

"Yeah, Mom, you're right. I just yelled at Phil and told him off."

I don't repeat the offensive words I used. Those would've shocked her.

"How did that go?"

"So cathartic. Really gooood."

I lift my head and blow my nose with a tissue.

Mom shifts sideways in the cuddle chair, tucking one leg under the other. "So, you're upset I left you at home."

"Well, logically, I see you had to work. But emotionally, that's a whole 'nother thing."

She nods vigorously. "Mm-hmm."

"I want to get rid of this once and for all. Please help me."

Mom's eyes search mine. "Now?"

I rub my forehead and blow out a puff of air while my fingers tap my lips. "Yeah."

She cups my face with her hands. "Describe your emotions. Don't hold back."

"Hmm. This isn't gonna be easy." I turn my head to study the floor and scoot back a bit. "Here goes . . . almost all my friends' moms stayed home, greeting them after school. You were never there."

I was a latch-key kid, except the city seemed safe, so we never locked our doors.

I think about how I envied the afternoon greetings in the TV shows. I had dreamed of bouncing into the kitchen, shoving a freshly baked cookie in my mouth, and Mom asking how my day went.

As if working all day wasn't enough, Mom directed and performed in plays at night. Or, she was busy reading. Even when she was there, she wasn't really *there*. All the time. Rejection. That's what jumps to mind. Abandonment, too.

"You left me defenseless, alone at home, so Phil could prey on me."

My hand rushes to cover my mouth. "Gosh, that seems harsh. I don't mean to attack you."

Much of the time, I wasn't actually alone because Dad or the older kids were home, but I wanted her most of all. Sometimes, we would do stuff together as a family, and she was always with us on Sundays, including at church.

Wonderful memories flit through my mind, including long talks.

"I love you so much, but . . . oh, damn. All this hurt and love get mixed together."

Tears flow as fast as my neck and cheeks redden.

Mom strokes my hair and dries my face. "Now, now. There, there. Don't worry. It's all right. You need to get this out."

I realize she couldn't stop Phil, even if she were home. Plus, it wasn't possible to protect me from everything. Logically knowing and emotionally accepting are two different things, though.

"Geez, Mom. I hated that you weren't around when I was little. But I did the same thing to my kids. Dammit. What kind of mother was I?"

I don't actually want her to answer and cringe.

Why do I keep punishing myself?

Then, it hits me: Phil. "Guess I believe I didn't protect *my* kids."

"You sure it's just about your kids?"

"What do you mean?"

"What about Beth?"

"Ooooh. Wow. You could be right. I mean, it kinda makes sense. Like, if *you* couldn't protect Beth, as an adult, *I* should."

"Right. So, forget rationality. Who do you blame?"

"Of course, it's all Phil's fault." I swallow hard before continuing. "And, yeah, if you'd been home . . . but I guess . . . I blame myself. Like, I was an idiot and should've known better. All sorts of 'I should've,' 'I could've,' and 'if only' torture me."

"For example?"

"Well, I shouldn't have trusted him. I didn't say no. I didn't say anything. But my whole body froze. I couldn't even open my mouth."

Again, I set off on a foolish mental race to figure out what I should've done differently.

Left after baking?

Not go with him?

Not let him "show me something?"

Logic interrupts.

I was taught to respect adults.

How would I have known better, at six?

How could I have predicted what he did?

Blame butts in.

Lifelessness in his eyes.

You should've . . .

"Dammit! This is so freakin' annoying."

Mom smooths my hair in three silken strokes, starting at my widow's peak and ending at the base of my neck.

"You need to forgive yourself. Get Beth."

3 BETH BECKONS

I promise I will protect you . . .

THE NEXT DAY, I swivel side to side in my writing chair while I ponder forgiveness. Not Phil's. Mine.

Visualizing Phil and chewing him out doesn't erase self-blame. Beth must still think she should have acted differently, too. I can't expect one round of emotional exorcism to succeed. She's been carrying this weight submerged in our psyche almost five decades.

Mom's right. To heal fully, I need Beth.

I close my lids and focus on my breath. Gentle tingles glide through my body and limbs. I allow my mind to drift until it catches a surge of inspiration.

⊂8∂

Along a shoreline, water pools in the imprints I leave behind after wet sand squishes beneath my bare feet. A dusky mauve and lavender sky shimmers ahead.

Tiny crabs scamper sideways into their holes, bracing for the next surf to slide nearer to its last foamy outline. The moist wind tickles my skin, both cooling and warming at the same time.

My newfound peace and serenity from healing my depression only spread so far. After digging up the details about Phil, Beth retreated to her childhood sanctuary, the cave.

I stand at the gaping mouth that swallows childhood emotions. As I slip into the inky cavity, my fingertips trace its jagged inner cheek. I pray for no nicks. My body shivers within the stone-cold atmosphere. Dry sand sticks to the bottom of my wet soles. I hope I won't trip on any boulders blocking my way.

I pause and remind myself to search for Beth through my heart instead of sight. I sense her cowering in a corner and reach out my hand. "You don't need to stay here anymore. I promise I will protect you."

She slips her tiny hand into my mature one. We turn toward the twilight beckoning outside. Arid sand gives way to damp warmth.

With the chasm behind us, we halt at its entrance and allow our irises to adjust.

A salty gust surges to greet us. Its intensity nearly sweeps us backward. Beth's grip tightens. I give her three squeezes of assurance.

"Let's begin."

CR&O

Beth and I visit our childhood home.

In the lazy summers, we kids carved out four-inch chunks from the turf to play makeshift golf games. Sometimes the grass cushioned our backs as we gazed skyward, imagining all the pictures the clouds painted for us. Planked remnants of an unfinished treehouse still scar the mature elm in the front yard. Now, its leaves shade smiling panes.

From the outside, the front window on our left flashes an eight-foot-wide grin. A narrow band of stained-glass teeth set the interior alight in colorful sparkles when rays catch it. Above it, rectangular eyes twinkle from the top story; the sashes in the middle serve as eyelids. To our right, a thick skin of white brick curves into a long-necked porch where we stow bicycles and Beth's red tricycle. Lilac bushes brush against rose trellises, each shading its cheeks. Red-shingled gables crisscross its crown.

The porch slats creak as we walk toward the front entry. A sheet of glass spans most of the door. Framed by walnut wood, curtains behind the glass veil our view from outside. We open the door and step onto the foyer's beige carpet. On our left, a white pocket door stands eternally open. Its floor-to-ceiling height makes it awkward to open and close. We pass through it to the parlor, always ready for visitors.

In front of us, two white couches sit perpendicular to each other separated by teak side tables, taupe lamps, and a teak coffee table. Since we don't drink coffee, we call it a Postum table. A cherub sconce hugs the wall above the couch, clasping faux flowers in lieu of lights.

We walk toward the middle, where a vintage brass chandelier dangles from the high ceiling. To our left, sheer curtains cover the grinning window, and drapes skirt each side. Squatting under the window, a white radiator waits for wintertime to dry our mittens or warm our hands.

We turn around. An enormous mirror hangs across the back wall, six feet wide and almost as tall, reflecting us and the rest of the room. Under the mirror stands a burnished brown piano. Beth points out her name carved into the upright. It was so enticing when she learned to spell; she couldn't resist. In the corner next to the piano, a presence draws our attention.

Azure eyes gaze at us. Under a pink derby hat, chestnut-colored hair curves around her face. Her smile surrounds us in a warm embrace. Her divine essence glides beyond the bounds of its antique frame hanging above the cuddle chair, and her portrait transfixes us: the grandmother we never knew.

When we sense another presence, we shift our attention to the doorway. Mom enters the parlor from the foyer. We greet her and settle into the cuddle chair to chat.

Beth snuggles between Mom and me, but she isn't ready to talk about Phil. Instead, she tugs on Mom's sleeve, leans back, and points at the portrait. "Mama, tell us about her."

4 MOTHER MARY

An angel on this earth . . .

"YOU KNOW, I painted your Grandma Mary this way because that's how I saw her. That's how everyone else saw her, too. Never uttered an unkind word. So sweet—everyone called her an angel on this earth. I put Mother on a pedestal. I suppose we all did."

I consider how Grandma died four years before I was born. I remember hearing since they were both named Mary, her family called Mom "Little Mary" to avoid confusion. Even when Mom was a teen and towered over her mother, she was still Little Mary.

Mom sighs and shrugs.

"I resolved to be like her. Instead, I turned out more like Dad. When I was young, I couldn't figure out why somebody so good-natured as Mother ended up with a man like Dad—but I'm getting ahead of myself."

Not sure what she means about Grandpa Rob, I furrow my brows for a second. But I let her continue without interrupting.

Grandma Mary and her older sister, Aunt Rachel, were bosom pals. Almost inseparable, they acted like twins but were eighteen months apart. When they were younger, they also looked alike with flaxen hair. Their parents held back Aunt

Rachel so she and Grandma could start elementary school together. Grandma was timid, and they wanted Aunt Rachel to look after her.

The sisters learned to sew in high school and served as apprentice seamstresses after graduation. The woman they worked for designed elegant gowns for wealthy women.

"Mother loved to sing in the church choir and taught Sunday school. I betcha didn't know she gave dramatic readings."

My mouth falls open. "What?"

"Yup, saved 'em all in a scrapbook."

This doesn't sound like Grandma to me. Sounds more like Mom. "I heard she was shy."

"Oh, she was. Mostly, she performed for the family. Her father encouraged her. But she yearned for more."

"Huh. Guess you got your acting bug from her."

"Maybe so, but listen to this." She winks at us, slides off the cuddle chair, and acts out all the roles in the next part of Grandma's story.

Originally from Ireland, Great-Grandpa Wills had straight, black hair and a ginger handlebar mustache. One day when Grandma Mary was in her late teens, he shaved off his mustache, threw on old clothes and a funny hat, slipped out the back, and rang the front bell. The only other person at home, Grandma was sewing in her room. When Grandma opened the front door, she didn't recognize this clean-shaven fellow. Great-Grandpa Wills exaggerated his Irish brogue.

Mom adds a lilt to her reenactment. "Sure, and I'm your father's cousin, Patrick O'Shaughnessy, from County Mayo."

"Patrick" asked if her papa was around, so Grandma Mary told the stranger to wait on the porch while she fetched her papa. She searched throughout the house and barn, but, of course, she couldn't find him. Meanwhile, Great-Grandpa Wills wandered inside and relaxed in the parlor, relishing in his amusement. Grandma became unnerved upon her return. This brazen Patrick snuck into the house uninvited and settled in her papa's favorite chair. Grandma fidgeted while Patrick chit-chatted away about Éire and wished for his cousin's quick arrival. She fretted over her papa's absence, wanting him to rescue her from this stranger.

Not long after, Grandma's younger brother came home, took one look at Patrick and said, "Pa, you shaved off your mustache." Grandma insisted the man was Cousin Patrick. Not ready to end his make-believe game, Patrick stayed silent until her little brother took a few strides and snatched the hat from Patrick's head. Now, Grandma recognized her dear papa, but by this time, she was nearly in tears. Great-Grandpa Wills had to console her before they could all join in a good laugh about his prank. (Simmerman 1980)

Beth giggles. I'm glad to see her brighten.

I'm wondering if Great-Grandpa Wills may have passed the entertainer bug to Grandma Mary.

Mom returns to the cuddle chair, catches her breath, and resumes.

Grandma Mary and Aunt Rachel shared a bedroom and long chats. Because they did so much together, they shared almost everything. They also became attracted to the same man—Grandpa Rob. They met through a cousin of his. He moved to their city after his discharge from the Navy.

I recall Grandpa Rob's high cheekbones, broad forehead, steel-blue eyes, and long jaw. I only knew him as old and bald, but I've seen pictures of his younger days when he had a full head of straight brunette hair. He was lean and tall his whole life.

Beth says, "I remember how Grandpa took a penny, blew it from his hand, made it fly around the room, and pulled it from my ear."

"Yup. He played the penny trick many times," I say.

Mom tussles Beth's hair and smiles. "Yeah, Grandpa Rob joked around, too. Great-Grandpa Wills wasn't the only one.

"Anyhow, Mother's parents rented out their rooms to earn extra money, and Aunt Rachel and Mother suggested Dad consider boarding in their home."

Shortly after Grandpa moved in, Aunt Rachel warned Grandma to keep away. Grandpa later admitted Grandma had attracted him more at first, but she wouldn't pay him any attention. Instead, Grandpa dated Aunt Rachel. Within a year after they met, Grandpa and Aunt Rachel married and had three children, my Aunt Gwen Uncle Bob, and Uncle Jack.

During the 1918 epidemic, Rachel caught influenza. Grandpa was a naval officer fighting in World War I but came home on shore leave. Still weak, Rachel died in his arms from pneumonia only a few days later. Grandpa buried her before he shipped out again. While he was offshore, Grandma Mary and her parents took care of his three motherless children.

After the war, Grandpa Rob and Grandma Mary dated until they married the next year. Grandma gave birth to three children as well—Mom followed by her two brothers, Uncle Donlon and Uncle Wendell. So, Grandma's and Aunt Rachel's kids followed the same birth pattern.

Mom winks at Beth. "Quite a coinkydink, some would say. Mother said people often commented on the fact that the three older children seemed alike, and the three younger children seemed alike, but they didn't seem very much like each other. She'd just smile and say, 'Yes, isn't that strange?'"

Grandma Mary loved Aunt Rachel's children as her own.

They were cousins, stepsisters, and stepbrothers, but never thought of each other that way. Mom's older sister and brothers treated Grandma as their own mother, too.

"Mother treasured family the most. Did what she could to keep it harmonious. But she couldn't fix everything."

Mom turns her attention away from Beth to me. "You're not the only mother with regrets. You're in good company. As much as we revered our mother, she wasn't perfect. We'll talk more about that later."

She looks back at Beth, "How do you like my stories so far?"

Beth beams. "Nice." Her smile turns into a frown. "That's so sad about Aunt Rachel. But thanks for telling me about Grandma, though."

Mom squeezes Beth around the shoulders. "You're so welcome. Think you're ready to talk about something else?"

Beth looks down and fiddles with her fingers. When she opens her mouth, nothing comes out but a sigh.

Mom's eyes flash. She pulls Beth closer and dots the tip of Beth's nose with her index finger. "Dr. Mom to the rescue."

5 NICE NEIGHBOR

A special sharing time . . .

"Let's play make-believe," Mom says. "Make up a fun story about following Phil upstairs. Keep some stuff the same but change anything yucky with something nicer. Can you try that?"

Beth's eyes plead with mine. "But you promised."

I pat her hand. "I'll be with you the whole time. Nobody but you will see me unless you want them to." I cradle one of her hands in both of mine. "If you get scared, we'll leave. I won't let him hurt you."

Beth slides her other hand from my wrist to my fingertips a few times. "Okay."

"Imagine a special sharing time with Phil coming from a happy place. Think about that and tell us a nice version," Mom says.

Beth scrunches her eyes and mouth for a minute. Her brows unfurrow and lips unpucker before she whispers an idea to me.

I chuckle.

She grins and scoots forward. "Mama, I'm ready."

After the baking, Mrs. Joren leaves Beth in the kitchen. I stay by Beth's side.

Phil strides in. "Hi, kiddo. Hey, I have a surprise to show you, but you need to head upstairs for it."

He runs up the stairs taking two at a time. Beth walks upstairs, trailing her hand along the banister's shiny wood.

Phil smiles at her from the top of the stairs. He's wearing the same white shirt and black pants. His raven mustache and hair match his pants. His straight hair ends above his collar and ears. He parts it on the side and keeps it slicked down with pomade. He taps his foot as if doing so will make Beth climb faster. But, she's with me, and I let her take her time. When we catch up, he leads the way to his room.

We pause at the threshold. I notice the walnut armoire and its matching four-poster bed frame. Beth yanks on my teal blouse with her free hand and looks up at me. I respond with a pump of reassurance and a grin. We walk to a multi-colored rug in the middle. It reminds me of the rugs Nana braided at my home.

Phil says, "What I'm gonna show you is a secret. Don't want my mama to know."

Beth nods. "I promise."

Phil opens the closet door and lifts a little brown furball from a box. It squirms and lets out tiny yaps. He urges Beth to touch it.

Beth lets go of my hand and strokes the puppy's back, ears, and nose. "Its fur is so soft."

I move to a corner near the dresser while she immerses in the scene.

Phil explains he found the puppy, but the mother dog had died. He doesn't believe Mrs. Joren will let him keep the pup if she finds out.

Beth frowns and wonders why a grown-up can't do what he wants, even if he lives with his mama.

Her attention returns to the puppy. "It's sure cute, though." The puppy licks and tries to suck Beth's finger. Phil points to a baby bottle filled with milk and asks if she wants to feed it.

She grins ear to ear and settles on the rug in her purple and white polka-dot dress and white, T-strap sandals. She sits cross-legged and cradles the puppy in her lap.

Her body wiggles as she nuzzles her cheeks against it and inhales its sweet, milky scent.

Phil waves the bottle in front of her until Beth snatches it. She tilts the bottle and places it in the puppy's mouth, watching its Adam's apple bobbing as it swallows.

While Beth feeds the puppy, she scans the room. She smiles at me and gazes at photos of Mr. and Mrs. Joren on the dresser. "Your mama's so nice. Baking with her is fun. Sometimes, being with her warms me all over, like opening an oven full of sugar cookies."

Phil beams and so do I.

A high-pitched slurping sound returns Beth's attention to the pup. An empty bottle. She puts the puppy on the floor to scoot around on its tummy and wobbly legs. Phil sits cross-legged, opposite her on the rug. We all enjoy the contented puppy's antics.

Phil explains why he keeps the puppy in the warm closet. Beth still wonders how he'll keep it a secret from his mama but shrugs her shoulders.

Unfortunately, Mrs. Joren calls for Phil. He opens the door to answer.

Beth frowns. "Aww, too bad. I gotta go home now."

She puts the puppy into its bed. "Thanks for showing me."

Beth bounces down the stairs. I can hardly keep up with her. Mrs. Joren approaches and asks Beth what she was doing upstairs.

Not wanting to snitch, she giggles. "Phil and I were just playing."

As she skips toward home, Beth says, "Can't wait to tell Danny about the puppy. He'll be sooo jealous, but he won't tattle."

I agree with Beth, her buddy will keep the secret, and the playtime fades.

We're back at the cuddle chair.

Beth looks at Mom. "Um, that's it."

"So, how do you feel now?"

"Kinda lucky . . . to have such a nice neighbor." Beth's face shines with as much cheer as the poppies by our driveway.

SUPPRESSING EXPRESSION

*Embedded those lessons about suppression,
oblivious to your body's cues*

6 WHAT ABOUT WOODY?

Her lifelong companion became "him" . . .

MOM AND I rest on the cuddle chair a few weeks later. She wears the same white suit and blue blouse, but her hair now gleams a creamy white. I love her eyebrows' high arches.

I clasp one hand together with hers and begin our little ritual. My other hand slides from Mom's wrist, over her knuckles to neatly trimmed nails and back again. It started as a soothing routine during boring church sermons in my childhood. As I continue on, tracing her visible veins across her smooth skin, I note a sprinkling of age spots.

My logical mind reminds me it's been over ten years since I did this in person, but my imagination doesn't mind. As I melt into the comforting sensations, memories of her illness flood me.

☙❧

"Liz, Mother is in the hospital. It's serious. The doctor said, 'Ask your family if they want to say goodbye because she may not last through the night.'"

My sister's words shoot through the receiver and explode

in my head, shattering all my other life concerns. Although Mom and I had periodically discussed the inevitability of final goodbyes, I'm not ready to let go without seeing her again. I focus on finding the next available flight.

Seated on the plane for the two-hour trip, the chilly window frame props up my weary head. Thoughts scatter as clouds across the sky. Jumbled memories and notions about a motherless future intermingle with my ceaseless and selfish prayer to please keep her alive, at least until I arrive.

I can't sign for the rental car fast enough. My mental map of the familiar city runs on autopilot as I navigate to the hospital. The reception area offers assorted comfortable seating. A Christmas tree glitters in one corner. I ask a greeter behind an oak counter for Mary Pederson's room number. She repeats Pederson but changes the first name to Woody.

"No, I want the room number for my mother, Mary."

Why would she say Woody? What's Dad got to do with her room number? Why can't this hospital keep things straight?

"He was admitted as well," she says.

I note the number and enough of the greeter's directions to the intensive care unit before dashing to the elevator. *Why's Dad in the hospital? What's wrong with him? Are both my parents going to die now, leaving me an adult orphan?*

I heave a welcome sigh when I spot my siblings in Mom's room. The staff wheeled Dad from his room to Mom's temporarily. They lie side by side in their respective hospital beds, hooked up to intravenous fluids and an oxygen mask for Mom. I always thought of Dad as a white-haired John Wayne. But contraptions dwarf both his six-foot-four-inch frame and Mom's five-foot, ten-inch figure. The frailty of Mom in her late seventies and Dad in his mid-eighties smacks me with a sudden realization of life's fragility.

Each sibling offers their piece for me to fit the whole picture together.

Soon after Mom and Dad celebrated Thanksgiving and their birthdays with my family in sunny Arizona, they returned to snowy Utah, and Dad caught what he thought was a common cold. After two weeks, he couldn't shake it off and grew worse, so Mom took him to the doctor's office. Wooziness knocked Mom off balance too, but intent on caring for Dad, she had ignored her symptoms. The doctor was more alarmed by Mom's condition than Dad's and rushed her to the intensive care unit via ambulance while Dad followed behind.

Tests confirmed pneumonia. Doctors also determined Mom had struggled for years with a limited lung capacity—now barely ten to twenty percent of normal. Specialists reasoned polio contracted in her early twenties weakened her lungs over decades to develop into bronchiectasis. This diagnosis finally explained her daily hacking bouts and coughing up small globs of phlegm ever since I can remember.

The physicians offered little reassurance. They doubted Mom could cling to life much longer, measured by the slivers of air she inhaled.

When the doctors asked Mom about resuscitation, she struggled to speak above a mumble. "I've done everything I've ever wanted to do."

Mom wobbled in and out of consciousness. My brother-in-law placed his hands onto Mom's head. He offered a prayer, seeking divine intervention for Mom to hang on long enough for those of us traveling to visit her. His inspired words offered Mom a choice: she could depart or remain, but if she remained, life would be completely different.

Mom opened her eyes.

Dad sagged beside her in a visitor's chair. "Mary, do you want to die?"

She glanced at Dad then regarded my sisters. "But what about him?"

She wasn't asking their opinion.

At the end of visiting hours, my exhausted family went home to rest and left her in God's hands.

Mom survived the night.

By morning, a raging fever weakened Dad. Aided by my brother-in-law, Dad doddered back to his doctor's office. This time, Dad's doctor also sent him to the hospital in an ambulance. By the time I arrived, both Mom and Dad were battling acute pneumonia.

I stand in Mom's room, fully grasp both Mom and Dad's withered condition, and wonder about the difference between Arizona's warmth and Utah's chill being a contributing factor. I conclude the extreme change in climate weakened their immune systems and sent them to the hospital. *If they hadn't visited me, they wouldn't be sick.*

It's my fault my parents are dying.

ඃ෮

A stroke claimed our mother.

In her place, we welcomed a feeble stranger. Relentless haze clouded her memory. At times, she didn't recognize her own children.

But Mom never forgot what happened after the family left the hospital that first night. She rose from her bed and traipsed along the intensive care unit's corridor. Physically, we knew she couldn't have left her bed, much less ventured outside her room. Maybe imagination carried her away or perhaps a brief brush with death did. Either way, I believe she chose life at that moment.

Mom's struggle to stay alive for Dad exacted a swift toll of deepened dementia. Doctors suspected her fragile lungs didn't deliver enough oxygen to her brain and triggered a series of mini-strokes.

She strained to select words which refused to surface. She permanently forgot Dad's name, so her lifelong companion became "him."

Before their hospitalization, Mom's memory loss had been a minor inconvenience. Her vast vocabulary had defined her writing and editing career and acting hobby. Now, these achievements abandoned her.

Within weeks after their hospitalization, Dad and Mom convalesced and resumed living in their condo community.

Despite macular degeneration and his inability until then to manage household bills and bank accounts, Dad became determined to care in every way for his dependent wife. He recorded meticulous checkbook entries and tallied the register, all magnified by a plate-sized lens. A few months later, he showed my sister his bank statement. She held power of attorney and mentored him in money matters.

He pointed to the figure for interest earned. "Did you know that if you just leave your money in the bank, they *pay* you for it?"

Dad and Mom kneeled in morning and evening prayers. While he prepared breakfast, she cleaned his hearing aids. Each day he counted his blessings and admired her through newlywed eyes, ending each night's prayer with a kiss.

Two years after their bout with pneumonia, doctors removed a tumor in Mom's tear duct, and took her sense of smell and taste buds with it. Savory food not only wafted odorless and smacked flavorless but also lingered unremembered. A portable oxygen tank pumped a steady supply, as much air as her delicate lungs could handle. Dad's legs swelled with excess fluid, making it difficult to wear shoes or exert himself. He missed expiration dates and subtle signs of food spoilage.

They made it through the mundane for eighteen more months, until Dad's daily duties as household administrator, chef, and nurse for Mom loomed monumental. He needed more support than his eighty-nine-year-old autonomy accepted. Despite Dad's constant care, Mom's svelte body shriveled to a ninety-pound skeleton. We bemoaned the amount of expired food we discarded from the kitchen shelves and fridge. Visits from home health aides and my sisters had not been enough. Two blondes and four brunettes regrouped after a reunion: my sisters Kathleen, Kristine, Yvonne and brothers Steven and Quintin, and me.

My sisters had already talked with Dad about options that included a live-in helper. Quintin had also told Dad he couldn't properly take care of Mom and needed to get her into an assisted living center. Although Dad said, "Okay," he hadn't taken action.

In Kristine's home, the six of us discussed our concerns about Dad and Mom living alone and various alternatives. Kathleen had already set aside a guest bedroom for them, but her full-time job and rural setting eliminated this as a viable option.

The six of us bowed our heads and kneeled around Kristine's king-size bed, seeking divine guidance and inspiration. As we appealed for wisdom, a calming presence filled our hearts. Unseen loved ones seemed in attendance, too.

Reassured, our rising faces shone, and various shades of

blue eyes splashed tears of love and compassion. We bonded in a group embrace.

We nominated Steven, as the oldest son, to have a follow-up conversation.

Steven encouraged Dad to move from their condo. Dad brandished blind tenacity about independent living. Dad insisted a retirement home or assisted living center meant putting one foot into the grave. Before her final retirement, Mom had scouted a comfortable senior community but deferred to Dad's wishes.

Our counsel sprouted within two or three months, after an illness triggered another hospital stay for Dad. Intent on resuming Mom's care and affirming his liberation, Dad insisted he would go home. He stood up to leave, wearing only a drafty hospital gown. Yvonne reminded him she had both his wallet and wife in her care. Dad relented. Within days, the doctor sent Dad to a recovery facility. Frustrated at his inability to attend to Mom from afar, he was glad when arrangements allowed her to stay with him while he recuperated.

During his stay, Dad's physician diagnosed and treated him for bipolar affective disorder, unlocking a brand-new explanation for a lifetime of personal and familial dysfunction.

When Yvonne mentioned Dad's recent money management skills to the doctor, he considered Dad's success extraordinary, since the doctor said Dad's bipolar disorder should have made it impossible.

As Dad's health strengthened, his resolve for independence weakened. He admitted we were right. Upon Dad's recovery, Mom and Dad resettled in Golden Living Center, the skilled care community Mom had chosen decades earlier.

Dad was known to strike up conversations with strangers at grocery check-out counters, so it was no surprise that at the

Center he made new friends. When he recited *The Lion and Albert* and *Albert's Return,* comedic poems he had watched Mom perform hundreds of times, we were surprised. However, Albert became Egbert and not one line of the quatrains rhymed, but he delivered the gist down pat. Mom laughed so hard at his substitutions, she fell off her chair.

Another time, the Center threw a crazy hat contest. Dad entered the competition with an improvised plastic grocery bag, fluffed to a poufy height and hooked around his lobes. As he related the story to me, he recreated the wacky hat with a clown's expressions to match. My belly ached from laughing. As I hugged my splitting sides, an irony tickled me. Mom and Dad's roles switched. He became the performer, and she was his audience.

We out-of-state children visited our parents when we could, but Yvonne assisted weekdays, and Kristine helped on weekends. We all missed our witty, word-maven mother, but the new one didn't nit-pick for perfection. Muted were her shrill shouts to catch Dad's deafened attention. Instead, Mom laughed at her language lapses, displaying grace in tragedy. Dad and Mom blended into one as she became his eyes and ears, and he acted as her memory.

Mom swapped words in a skewampus autocorrect style. We adapted to her lexicon and translated, weaving meaning from terms she strung together. One day, she explained how family remained most important to her. She cherished her six children and husband as her greatest desire and source of joy. After five decades with Dad, life blessed her with serene contentment. Although she clung to life for him, she reached a new level of readiness. "Whenever the Lord wants to take me," she said, "I am ready to go . . . uh . . . boom."

They each received gifts from misfortune. Dad found gratification as Mom's constant protector, in his newfound money management skills, and theatrical talents. Elusive riches he had pursued to prove his worth and earn our family's love gave way to a wealth money could never buy. Mom sought solace in her gentlest nature. Our new mother shimmered as a gem of unconditional love.

Destiny granted Mom her lifelong aspiration: attaining her mother's saintly qualities. In the Golden Living Center, our earth angel sparkled as the sweetest jewel for another year and a half.

൙൚

When they met after World War II, it was love at first sight for Dad. He had noticed Mom's picture posted on a church bulletin board. Brunette victory rolls framed her face. Her movie-star mien in the glamor shot captivated him. He resolved to rendezvous.

For Mom, meeting Dad was more measured. She had noticed him at a dramatic reading where she performed. In her words, she spotted a "long, slim drink of water" entering the room. With wavy, strawberry-blonde strands complementing his ruddy complexion, his chiseled physique cut a fine figure in his double-breasted suit. They weren't introduced until later, though. Mom's friends pointed him out at a dance. He stood at the entrance to the recreation hall where Mom noticed the outside light shone on him like a halo on a Norse god.

Her friend nudged her. "Oh, he looks tall enough for you."

She licked her lips a little. "Yeah." (Whitworth 2008)

At her height, she kept an eye out for such rarities.

Throughout the night, they danced polkas, fox-trots, and jitterbugs. When he asked to escort her home, she explained she lived next-door, so he proposed a longer route via a soda shop.

She'll narrate what came next.

Mom's History/Diary: Excerpt One

I had to take home a lot of stuff, so we stopped by my house, and then Woody took me downtown to Snelgrove's. We had a malt, and as we sat there, Woody started telling me all about his family. I thought, *Blah, blah, blah.*

I wasn't one bit interested. I figured when I got home, I'd never see him again.

He says, "You know, my family all think I'm an old batch; they sure kid me about it all the time."

I thought to myself, *Boy, this guy is so set on getting married, he'll marry anybody! Well, it isn't going to be me!*

Then, I knew.

A little, inner voice in my head whispered, *Oh, yes, it is! He's the one.*

So, I thought I'd better pay more attention. (Whitworth 2008)

When they met in mid-February, Dad was thirty-four and Mom twenty-six. He appeared sincere but too desperate. The dawning impression he was "the one" shocked her. Although conflicted by the notion, her confidence intensified as she pondered, reflected, and prayed. Engaged by their third date, they married three months later, in early May.

Dad adored Mom and her many gifts. His high regard placed her on a pedestal for us to revere which is why we called her Mary Poppins, practically perfect. She was not an impeccable wife and mother, but we idolized the idea. Her depth and breadth of talents also made her seem almost perfect in every way.

Growing up, I didn't hear my parents argue, but they didn't agree on everything. I later discovered the main reason for superficial smoothness: Mom suppressed her feelings about many issues, simmering in silence.

Repressing expression has been happening for generations.

7 SORROWFUL SURRENDER

I soak in remembrance . . .

Grandma Mary didn't complain to her girlfriends. She didn't nag her husband, Grandpa Rob. Shushed as a youngster, she turned inward. Besides, Rachel had always been her spokesperson. Grandma expressed herself in private, where she poured her heartbreak to the Lord. She presumed whatever the Lord allowed she could deal with and accept. She did her best to live a life of surrender.

Mom did not meet this ease in her life until the dementia-induced transformation. Her siblings claimed she got away with more than they did. As a teen, Mom would rush household chores so she could read a book, perform in a play, or immerse in other entertaining activities.

Mom feigned laughter at her father's jokes, but his underlying harsh tone pricked her. Grandpa Rob didn't note her sensitivity or his impact on his children. He never saw his high expectations as anything out of the ordinary. When Grandpa fled from home at eighteen and covertly enlisted in the Navy, he thought he had escaped his dad's domination. He had traded one autocratic form of command and control for another.

In turn, Grandpa ran a tight domestic ship, barking commands and growling about deviations from his charted course. This tactic made any form of fatherly criticism a crushing burden for Mom. She bristled but submerged her sentiments inside.

Mom's History/Diary: Excerpt Two

In many ways, I was emotionally deprived and not allowed to accept or express my feelings. I know I was never taught how to deal with them, and I think my brothers and sister may have looked upon me as a crybaby. I didn't know any other way to express disappointment or hurt—had never learned to verbalize feelings.

Eventually, I learned to shut them off, or when possible, go up to my room, sit on the bed, and have a good cry. I remember doing that when I was fifteen. Dad was always hurting our feelings, and I had determined to not let him see when he hurt me. But there was a lot of buried anger and hurt . . . I couldn't rely on my father to be affectionate and supportive, but he did give a stability to our life . . . I resolved to be like my mother, who was an angel on earth, yet, I became a sharp-tongued critic like Dad. (Whitworth 2004)

Mom wearing a mask onstage was easier than exposing her vulnerability offstage. She struggled to claim her authentic voice throughout much of her life. In her eighties, Mom could no longer articulate because her brain denied access to words. However, she gained peaceful acceptance of her past and present. This gave her the new ability to offer unfettered love.

Until I read her diary, I didn't realize Mom sat sobbing alone in her room as a teenager. I did that, too. I guess a tendency to stifle my emotions passed from Grandma Mary to Mom to me. My inner storms formed in stealth and burst much to my surprise.

I recall one unexpected squall from my mid-forties.

The Light Within

☙❧

I sit among the back rows in the dim conference hall with 250 other company leaders. Movie clips playing on the front screen emit the only light. A collage of motivational moments, the snippets serve as our final pep rally to reverse plunging revenues. I watch but don't absorb the presentations.

My head pounds in my right temple. I suffer this non-stop stabbing once or twice a month. My doctor calls them cluster headaches because, unlike migraines, mine last three days. They cause involuntary teardrops and my right lid droops during the attack. It batters my stomach with nausea. My entire body tenses under pressure. The throbbing behind my socket pulses with my heartbeat and matches the intensity of a knife wedged in the knot under my right shoulder blade. Altitude sickness at this ski resort intensifies everything. The perfect storm adds to the mix my menstruation flowing fiercer than usual, with cramps and a backache battering me, too.

I stare past motivational movie clips and into mental bedlam about tomorrow's presentation. My gut churns and tightens as I fixate over how to explain top management's new bonus plan. I've done most of the calculations, double-checked the charts, and fine-tuned for clarity. Tom Hanks's voice startles me when he bellows something from a *Saving Private Ryan* scene. I face the screen, but something else catches my attention.

I realize it's not anything Hanks says. It's the overlaid music sprinkling a foggy familiarity across me. As the tune intensifies, I soak in remembrance and transport back in time.

Another scene plays in my mind outside this auditorium. Words accompany the melody now. My daughter Victoria's voice floats acapella in front of the audience. Fragrant sprays of flowers adorn each side. Behind her rests Mom's wreathed casket. Although Mom is part Irish, this is not the main reason Victoria chooses *O Danny Boy*. Through the lyrics, Victoria stands as Mom's surrogate to serenade Dad.

My memory flashes forward a few months. Again, Victoria stands tall and trim near a casket while sable ringlets bounce above her shoulders and her coloratura soprano rings in the rafters with her haunting rendition of the ballad. This time, she's honoring Dad's prior request to repeat the song at his funeral.

I sink in the pew with tissue in hand for my runny nose and tears. Beside me, my husband Gillis supplies a sturdy and comforting squeeze when I need it most. His ebony-black kinks form a perfect coif complemented by his mocha complexion. Weak, I rest my head on his shoulder. Our teenaged sons, Kenneth and Christopher, sit beside us, caramel combinations of Gillis and me.

During my tribute, I reminisce about Dad's sweet sawdust scent from house building and his influences in constructing our character.

Other vignettes from the two funerals flash through my mind flooding the present as I sit in the auditorium. My mental dam bursts in real-time.

They're gone.

Before long, I can't sniff the snot back fast enough. I sense a deep ache rising from my solar plexus, expanding into my heart and gut. A surge almost overpowers me. I subdue it, but need to flee this room before the next wave crests.

Can they tell?

Oh, God, don't let anyone see me.

They can't watch me fall apart.

I navigate through the conference hall haze and slip out the double doors. My tongue tastes salt, mucus coats my throat, and my cheeks glisten with wetness. I huddle over and cup my hand. Ooze from my nose pauses at my upper lip before dribbling to my palm.

Eww. I need tissues.

Lids downcast, the marbled carpeting blurs throughout the corridor.

Please, please, please, make me disappear.

Whoa, thank God, nobody I know.

Gotta get out of here.

Elevator.

Momentary relief rises as I hide within the four steel walls and press the button for my floor. I slump for support against a side and brace my weight on the rail with one hand while the other catches my dribbles.

As soon as the doors ding open, I rush down the hallway and escape behind my room's mahogany door. Now, safe and out of sight, I blow into the blessed tissues and wipe below my nose.

As the second tsunami rises, I snatch the whole tissue box and belly flop across the bed. Everything left unsaid blubbers from my lips.

"I love you.

"I miss you.

"I wish I had spoken at your funeral, Mom.

"I'm glad we got to say goodbye, Dad.

"Mom, I miss talking to you . . ."

Over the next thirty minutes, I carry on my one-sided conversation. Sobs, snot, and shouts purge the grief, finally mourning and releasing last year's losses.

When exhaustion engulfs me, my swollen eyes slumber.

8 RELUCTANT REMORSE

Choke on my big, fat fib . . .

GUILTY SCENES AND pain from my past seem to be what I seek out these days to explore and heal even when I'm not writing. One day, I'm flipping through my photo collection and pause at Danny's picture. I remember a side of me I would rather not share.

Friends as well as cousins, Danny and I were closer agemates growing up than any other kids in our neighborhood. Somehow his sandy-blonde hair always lost its part, fell over his brown brows, and hid his amber eyes. His pale complexion and black-rimmed glasses suggested studious geek. But you would rarely find his nose in a book. He was an outdoor explorer. I used to trail behind him as he hiked surrounding hills and mountain paths. I envied the camping adventures he described. He and his scout troop would pitch tents by bonfires under milky-way ceilings.

As adults, circumstances distanced us.

This particular day, we're returning from a family reunion and happen to book the same flight. From my center seat, my attention roams beyond Danny through the rounded windows to our right. The clouds' contours evoke the silhouettes of childhood sentinels and momentarily take me back.

From my usual spot in the back seat of the family car, I admired two felines sculpted from white stone. We always drove by them on our way to church. Resting regally on their haunches, they purred constant comfort to me. The cat carvings sat on opposite sides of the road. Behind the statues, trees formed an overhead arc with their boughs before merging into a woodland. Blurred sunlight streamed through openings in the leafy lattice, splashing the path below.

I shift gears from the past. "Remember those huge cat statues? I just saw clouds shaped like them."

We talk about how we must have passed by those statues hundreds of times. Danny tells me he dropped by the old neighborhood not so long ago. The statues still guard the canyon entrance.

"They must've seemed ginormous when we were kids. Each sit nearly nine feet tall," he says.

I mention how as a child I had the constant impression those cats protected me. As I grew up, the notion faded and so did my memory of them. I wasn't even sure the statues were real, anymore. "Does that ever happen to you?"

"Well, I have a pretty good recall, but I get what you mean."

We talk about my memories of a basement apartment my folks rented for a few months when we moved to Utah. I was only four, but I remember slipping through a bathroom cupboard into my bedroom. The setup was so strange. For many years, I thought it must have been a dream, but Mom assured me I remembered correctly.

My memory must be better than I give myself credit for. But I'm dancing around with all these diversions. I want to forget what I did to Danny seven years ago.

I look out the window again, scanning for more cumulus clouds. My fingers have a mind of their own and search for imaginary pimples to pop near my left ear. The engines hum a veil of audio privacy. I wonder whether today I can clear my conscience.

With a lopsided grin, he breaks our silence. "You know, funny how we only see each other at family reunions nowadays."

I feign a chuckle and mumble an excuse about why I don't make the drive to his house in the town next door. The real reason sears my underbelly.

I swallow intensifying saliva. My thumb and first two fingers rub together trying to remove invisible dirt from their tips. Still not sure why I spat wildfire years ago, I decide to come clean. "Sometimes there's the opposite: something we wish was just a dream, but it's real. More of a nightmare, I guess. Like the day you brought Jane over to meet me, and I totally lost it."

He twitches as the whole ordeal seems to flicker through his face.

Red-hot splotches cover my neck and rush to my cheeks. "I'm really sorry about what happened. I shouldn't have exploded."

A specific phrase roars through my mind before I banish it again. "I was still upset from the day before. I don't remember exactly what I said," I lied, "but I know it was horrible. I hurt you so much. I'm so sorry, Danny."

I nearly choke on my big, fat fib. Maybe he won't notice.

Before the memory spreads too far, Danny shrugs and stares at the cabin ceiling. "Yeah . . . it's okay. I know you're sorry. But you should apologize to Jane. It'd mean a lot to her."

He shifts his gaze to me and gauges my reaction.

"Mm-hmm." I don't say aloud, *Why tell your wife I'm sorry? Why would I apologize to her for something I did to you?*

I try to push away my promise and my lie.

Instead, my hollow promise stokes seven more years' regret to smother.

As I prepare for my overseas move, clearing clutter, discarding debris, and tying up loose ends, I shed emotional baggage as well. I can't stifle smoldering dishonesty anymore. I need to apologize to Jane and admit lying to Danny before I can move on.

I call Danny and confirm a good time to stop by. On the way, I consider how Jane and I never bonded. No wonder. She met me at my worst: a fire-breathing Chimera.

Danny escorts me into the living room. We exchange courtesies. I consider Jane's emerald eyes and waist-length, garnet hair. She doesn't seem to grasp why I'm here. My heart thumps throughout my neck and head. A giant aquarium bubbles in the background as I squeeze air in and out through my own filter.

She probably still thinks I'm a heartless bitch.

We sink into a brown leather sofa. Jane settles on one side of Danny, and I, on the other. I explain the reason I'm visiting and how sorry I am for my atrocious behavior many years ago.

Jane accepts my apology but claims it's not necessary. I consider getting clarification, but her expression stays glassy smooth.

A pointless trip.

My attention shifts to Danny, and his reddened face explains everything. He needed to hear me recant in front of Jane because that's how I had pounced on him.

I suck in strength to unload my big whopper. "Danny, I

told you I didn't remember the horrible things I said, but I can never forget the worst thing I screamed at you. I told you—"

"It's okay; you don't need to repeat . . ."

"I wish I'd never said it."

Danny tilts his head and slips his hand in mine.

My chest lets out a soft exhale.

We each sit nearly nine feet tall.

9 FOOTSTEPS TO FOLLOW

Generational motherhood guilt . . .

Later, I reflect on the early phase of Mom's work life and hobbies. She held many positions over the years. Her first notable stint involved a radio station during World War II. Mom created live broadcast sound effects, portrayed personalities, and wrote promotional spots.

After marriage, she switched between being a stay-at-home mom and working outside the home. When the money Dad made in his construction business and entrepreneurial pursuits wasn't enough to care for six children, she supplemented his income using her secretarial skills.

Stage-struck almost from infancy, Mom dreamed of becoming an actress. When she was little, an older cousin from California visited the family. Mom's cousin promised to carry her with him to Hollywood, stowed in his suitcase. Ready to start her acting career, she sobbed when he left without her. Her involvement in the movie industry waited for decades. Meantime, the stage summoned her.

In her teens, she became dear friends with Luacine, who shared her delight for storytelling. They formed a troupe called the Pickwick Players, producing, directing, and performing in many community theater shows. Mom told us how she played

Jo in *Little Women*, her favorite role, the evil stepmother in *Cinderella*, and others. She relished character roles.

When I was a child, she held a volunteer position as the drama director for our church district. Dramatic performances and other church assignments often kept her away in the evenings. I resented her job commanding attention all day and church work stealing her at night.

When she could, she took us with her. We had fantastic fun in the theater. The opportunity to grow up around the stage allowed us an expressive outlet. However, I didn't learn how to appropriately recognize and communicate my emotions at home, particularly distressing ones.

♾

I want to resume discussions with Mom, so I slip into my writing chair, shut my eyes, and breathe into the cuddle chair's imagery.

Mom tucks my hair behind an ear as we lounge in the parlor.

"Sorry I haven't visited so much lately, Mom, but I've been editing *From the Shadows*."

"I know, sweetie. It's okay that our discussions have been less frequent. You need to finish it. That opens the way for all your other books and healing to happen."

I brighten. "Thanks for your patience."

I'm not sure where this conversation will lead, but I want to hear everything, so I welcome another deep breath to better connect with her.

Mom talks about how her family struggled with finances when she was little, during the Great Depression of the 1920s to

1930s. During the times Grandpa couldn't find jobs, Grandma became the mainstay and switched to full-time work after all the kids were school age.

"I enjoyed spending time at my grandmother's, so I don't begrudge Mother working. Usually, I immersed in my adventure land, anyway, so being at Grandma Wills's place just meant I could let creativity roam."

Although Mom didn't resent her mother working, I wonder aloud whether Grandma may have been uneasy about it. Religious and social pressure created conflict within me. So, I figure during Mom and Grandma's child-rearing years, it must have been more stressful for them. We discuss how our church leaders regularly admonished women to stay home and rear children as a devout duty.

Mom nudges her bangs away from her eyes. "Well, I had enormous guilt. I betcha Mother did, too."

I've heard that generational emotions and trauma can pass to descendants, so I float an idea with Mom. Maybe she absorbed Grandma's unexpressed motherhood guilt and mixed it with her own. Then, I took some of Mom and Grandma's collective guilt and blended it with mine. Obviously, Mom's beliefs affected all of us kids, but we each reacted through unique experiences.

My mind returns to the time I hit rock bottom. "Maybe, for me, everything built up to a critical point, and generational motherhood guilt crested in me—"

"You think that's what happened?"

"Well, it could explain a lot, like wanting to kill myself over it."

Mom rubs her chin. "Ah. The perfect storm. Or, maybe the *perfection* storm." She winks and we both chuckle before she continues.

"But you know, it doesn't matter where your guilt came from. You can heal it, regardless. Let's focus there. Follow me."

We leave the parlor, and Mom opens the front door. I stand at the threshold and wonder where the yard went. *Maybe this is like moving in dreams.* A rectangular table stands in the center of a small room. The edges of the walls, floor, and ceiling blur together in a glow, so they appear rounded. Three translucent globes glow from the table's midsection. Smaller than bocce balls but larger than billiard balls, I guess they're about three inches around. The first ball shines white with a small sun's magnificence. The second one gleams obsidian black, sucking the light as a black hole. Akin to butterscotch-fudge-ripple ice cream, the third ball swirls light and dark.

Mom explains the white sphere glows with love. The obsidian one feeds on fear. The third sphere blends the other two. As I focus on the love ball, the blended ball brightens. When I look at the fear ball, the blended ball darkens.

I estimate the white ball weighs one pound and pick up all three. I juggle them, passing each up and down in crisscrossed loops. Love on my left, a blend on my right, and fear high above then switching places. I continue until my pace completes several cycles.

Each carries a distinct weight, making smooth sets more complicated. I slip up, dropping the blend and love balls, catching only fear, the heaviest. When I peer into fear's midnight patina, my heart pounds rapid-fire about the future and the past.

Mom encourages me to describe my physical reaction.

"A vice grips my solar plexus. My back and shoulder muscles tighten. My teeth grit and clamp shut. My brows furrow and eyes narrow. Each heartbeat shoots spikes of adrenaline everywhere. I'm armoring for battle with an invisible enemy."

"How can you change that?"

I set the fear globe on the floor. Instead, I cup the translucent love ball and wait for its influence.

"When I peer into love's center, I discern prismed traces of a rainbow inside. My core warms. My muscles loosen, and posture softens. My jaw relaxes and lips part to drink cool air. I sense an openness to future possibilities."

"What's related to fear?"

I shrug. "Anxiety, guilt, and shame."

"What do you attach to them?"

"Well, anxiety stirs up imperfection, and shame or guilt provokes unworthiness," I say.

"On the other hand, what about love? What do you think of?"

"Love evokes compassion, acceptance, and inspiration."

Mom concurs and explains the sensations are somatic responses. Our bodies send messages to our minds. How we relieve discomfort depends on how closely we listen to the promptings.

"You tend to use what you learned as a child. You watched the ways your dad and I interacted and how I stifled emotions. Subconsciously, you embedded those lessons about suppression, oblivious to your body's cues."

We recollect the family counseling Mom and Dad went through when I was in elementary school. From time to time, she would repeat a key thing she learned, such as I couldn't change someone's action, but I could change my reaction. It was good guidance, but even so young, my patterns had already formed. I didn't understand her advice's real power. Later, as an adult, I had grasped the significance intellectually, but in the emotional whirlwind of the moment found it difficult to put into practice. Now, she's expanding the idea to inner dialog.

She goes on to tell me I'm by no means stuck repeating the pattern forever. Through practice, I can become aware and attune to somatic sensations in pivotal moments. I can create more and more opportunities to choose a conscious response and decide which sphere to carry.

Mom motions to the table. "We'll set the balls aside for now."

I place them in their original spots.

"Give these ideas time to sink in while you look at more of your motherhood issues, sweetie."

But I'm not ready to look at my problems. Instead, once I open my eyes, I flip through papers in my writing room and read from Mom's diary.

10 MOTHERHOOD MALAISE

Groping my way to the light . . .

WHEN SHE WAS thirty-seven, two months after Quintin was born, and three years before my birth, Mom decided to pursue a full-time job.

Mom's History/Diary: Excerpt Three

Almost twenty years later! I've been too busy, it seems, to write down some of the thoughts and experiences I have had . . . It is hard to believe so much time has elapsed . . . I am glad I found this old diary. There are times when I almost forget who I am or how I came to be what I am, as I seem to have made such a complete break with the past.

I seem to be groping my way to the light all over again to find out where I fit in this new existence since I've been married. I've had some hard and bitter lessons to learn, but I am sure each experience has caused me to grow in understanding and, perhaps, wisdom. I do hope so. Perhaps if I will keep up this writing, I can relieve my mind of the pressures that so often build up in me. Having no one to talk things out with anymore keeps me from getting a very clear perspective of my problems. Perhaps writing them down will take the place of those old heart-to-heart talks with Luacine, Annie, Mary Beth and the others. It is taking me a long, long time to make independent decisions and judgments . . .

I never dreamed that marriage and children would have to displace all that I once had. Yet, if I were offered the choice, I know I would retain what I have now. I did not realize my unused talents and abilities would nag at me so—and there never seems to be enough time. I feel so rushed so constantly. Not that I am so busy accomplishing things, but that I can do only one thing at a time, and I seem to barely get through the necessary duties, let alone have time for what I would like to do.

I am praying for guidance now. Does a mother really have to stay home all the time and devote herself strictly to homemaking in order to raise her children properly? I would do nothing to diminish my children's growth and development, and if I knew for *sure* that was the *only* answer, I think I could be content. The First Presidency has reiterated the Church stand on this time and again . . . But I wonder if allowance is made for our individual differences. Men are encouraged to find work suited to their talents, physical abilities, and disposition! Are women any different? Not all women are happy in the arts of homemaking—is that a necessary adjunct to the welfare of our children? Must I do all the work myself, by hand, or is it enough for me to oversee the home management and leave myself enough time and energy for constructive leisure with my children?

I sometimes feel my children are more neglected when I am home, as I am too busy or distracted with all these duties to listen to them properly—or else I am away on

The Light Within

a church assignment, leaving them alone. At least when I am at a business, I can afford to hire a sitter to watch over them.

As I recall the scriptures concerning women, we are advised to comfort and assist our husbands and sustain them in their callings and to teach our children the gospel . . . I am not doing it properly now. Will I do it any better if I work away from home during the day? The Lord has blessed us each time I have done it, with women who are congenial and loved by our children. Does this mean He approves or is just giving what assistance He can to a bad situation?

It is true I tire of being away from the children constantly and rejoice when I can quit work and stay home with them. I suppose I could stay home constantly and happily if there were not always the problem of our unpaid bills. Woody feels that eventually, things will work out so these can be paid . . . Perhaps I am too obsessed with being in debt and let it color everything out of proportion. It is a cross I am bearing very ungracefully. Yes, I find it does help to get these things out of my system onto paper.

. . . Well, all this is just one more interruption to the day. Breakfast dishes still not washed, missed a church meeting this morning, a washing to hang out, clothes to get ready for the girls' school program tonight, baby to bathe, another church program to check up on, and here it is noon.

I also have an appointment this afternoon with the county school superintendent about a job. I have about decided to take it, if it is offered me—supposing I can get a capable housekeeper. I hate to leave home, but I am never satisfied being here all the time—and part-time work means too many complications for babysitting and housework, and doesn't pay as much. Oh, woe is me. I can find as many cons on the other side of the ledger as I can pros. (Whitworth 2004)

My thoughts tie Mom's unease to her earlier reference about Grandma Mary's conflict and other details. Is it just my imagination, or has Mom been telling me things about Grandma I would have no way of knowing before? Whatever's happening, talking to Mom immerses me in delight. Would it work for Grandma, too?

I relax in my writing chair, close my eyes, and breathe deeply. When I return to the parlor, I picture Grandma joining me.

Grandma stands more slender than Mom. White curls halo her head, ending just below her ears. Bordered by arched brows she's probably never needed to pluck, her eyes shine with a summer sky's color and warmth. Her upper lip draws a thinner line than her fuller bottom, and her jawline forms the same half-oval I've inherited.

I see where Mom inherited her beauty.

"Grandma, I'm so excited to talk with you." I throw my arms around her.

"My dear, I am as well." She returns my embrace and leaves her hands on my shoulders while she takes a step back to take a good look at me. "You've been rehashing your misgivings and reading about your mother's worries awhile. Permit me to highlight some of mine."

Grandma eases onto the cuddle chair and taps the spot next to her for me to sit on. She describes how neither my uncle Bob nor Grandpa Rob seemed to interact for long without hurting each other. She suspected Uncle Bob and Grandpa Rob never bonded because Uncle Bob bore a resemblance to Grandpa Rob's father.

Over the decades, Grandma hinted to Grandpa Rob, but never insisted about what she wanted. She pleaded with the Lord to lift her load.

Aside from issues with family harmony, another yoke hung over Grandma. Similar to many other women laboring for employers during the Great Depression, Grandma trudged from home to job and back, six days a week.

Grandpa Rob's sales jobs allowed him flexibility to swing home once or twice during the day to check on their children, ensure chores ran on schedule, and prepare lunch. Unfortunately, sales didn't supply a steady salary. The older children tended the younger ones, and Great-Grandma Wills watched the kids when she moved next door. Grandpa found ways to stretch dollars by turning the morning's cracked-wheat mush into noontime's gruel by thinning it with canned milk, water, sugar, and vanilla. Sundays were Grandma's days off, so she cooked traditional meat and potatoes dishes.

Sewing in the alterations department wasn't a high-paying job, but it was a regular paycheck. Their six kids always needed something, but they never lacked necessities. At Christmas, Mom unfailingly unwrapped a new doll, not the fancy kind of her dreams.

Although Grandma yearned to stay home, working seemed a necessary part of life. She didn't assume she had any right to complain. Her sister Rachel had been better at expressing those kinds of thoughts, anyway.

Grandma chuckles. "I expect your mother learned to suppress her feelings through my example."

"Yeah, I guess so. Modeling behaviors and passing them down play a powerful role. I remember one sisters' get-together with Kathleen, Kristine, Yvonne, and me. We talked about how we dealt with distress. A couple of us joked, 'How did we learn to deal with emotions growing up? We *didn't*.'"

"I understand." She smiles, reaches for my hand, and strokes it. "As you recall, my papa emigrated from Ireland. Legend claims leprechauns hid a pot of gold at the rainbow's end. Although mythical, there's an element of truth."

Grandma explains how rainbows emerge when misty droplets in the skies separate white light rays into different hues. Each of us forms a droplet in a rainbow. Together, we paint a dazzling arc of red, orange, yellow, green, blue, indigo, and violet.

Yet, these colors all come from a unified source of white light—the sun—and we all emerge from a collective power.

As if on cue, sunlight streams through the window's stained glass and dances on the wall in all the colors Grandma described.

She gestures from the window toward the wall. "This shared power is the fabled treasure. It's available when we tap into the inner part of us. We may not see it, but we can always call on a profound connection to the Lord. Strength comes from a healing white light of unconditional love."

As the cuddle chair fades, I return my awareness to my writing room. I contemplate Grandma's reminder of God's divine essence within everyone and remember a childhood friend, Johnny.

PASSIONS AND POISONS

Something about the way he blathers sends a subtle shudder through Frances

11 JOHNNY'S JEWEL

Unconditional love . . .

ONLY A FEW children lived in our neighborhood. My family joked the residents were either "newlyweds or nearlydeads." Thanks to Danny, I enjoyed grand childhood adventures, nonetheless.

To us, Johnny was just one of the kids, but if he forgot to shave, his square jaw would cast a shadow by late afternoon. Johnny's loose mop of medium-brown hair spilled over razor-short sides. Brown puppy eyes lit up over life's little fascinations. A curly forest extended along his arms to his wrists with sprigs on his knuckles. He was the hairiest person I had known.

I remember coins clinking in his pockets. He would dip his hand, grin ear to ear, and count out his palmed treasures.

Johnny lived with his mother. The rumor mill said he suffered brain damage, but I never knew the details. Not allowed to cross the street alone, he pedaled around the block on his beloved bike for hours at a time. He seemed to savor the same boundless joy each trip.

I don't recall Johnny staying angry at us, even though we sometimes poked fun at his expense. He vented frustrations but would still give us a huge grin the next time we hung out.

One day, somebody snuck Johnny's bike and hid it from

him. The loss distressed Johnny, but when he found it almost danced with delight.

The way I remember him, Johnny unconditionally accepted everyone he met. If he carried a grudge, I never saw it. I always think of him with great fondness. I've heard parents of special needs children remark about what incredible love and forgiveness their kids can exude. I figure these children offer much we can learn from. You could say they demonstrate daily treasures from the rainbow.

I suppose all kids show these qualities. My children taught me much about unconditional love, but for decades I struggled to offer this same love to myself. Perhaps as we mature, we lose that childlike gift.

I envy Johnny's innocence, but admire his talent to value and expect the best in people. What a precious jewel he offered.

I want to be more like Johnny. I hope practicing forgiveness will help me find a way.

12 PERSNICKETY PASSION

I am the least-suspected creative . . .

MOST DAYS, I start with a blank slate about what I'll write. Even while I'm typing, I'm not always sure what I've written until I read it afterward. I usually close my eyes and allow inspiration to pour through. My fingers click up to one hundred words per minute, so I don't process all of it consciously.

An unusual murk veils today's topic. I shift position in my writing chair several times, breathe, and play Christopher's music anyway. After my mind and fingers float aimlessly within the fog a few minutes, I remember Victoria's question after reading a *From the Shadows* draft. "Mom, why didn't you say why it's such a big deal you started writing? I don't think your readers have any idea." My fingers quicken with clarity.

Victoria reminded me about a time in her early teens. In the adjoining family room, a newscaster thrummed on as evening entertainment while Victoria, Kenneth, Christopher, and I gathered around the kitchen's circular, smoked-glass table. We imagined all the possibilities about what they might do when grown.

Victoria said, "Mom, what's *your* passion?"

By then, I had left my corporate job and joined Gillis in the technology company we created.

"I don't have a passion. I help your Dad with his."

Another time, friends visited and admired the many watercolor landscapes, still-life sketches, and portraits on our walls.

My chest puffed as big as a peacock spreading its magnificent tail. "My mom and sister Yvonne are the artists."

I continued by emphasizing what a talented family I belonged to. After boasting about my five older brothers' and sisters' gifts, I cracked my usual joke. "As the youngest in the family, I figure I didn't inherit any creativity, because nothing was left over." I didn't bemoan the loss since I couldn't mourn what I never had. I resigned to this idea as a fact.

Victoria also urged me to paint a picture of how a pragmatic me ended up publishing poetry and stories. In high school, I studied transcription, shorthand, and typing, not creative writing. At work, I poured my efforts into practical business pursuits and half-heartedly climbed the corporate ladder to the senior management rung.

I am the least-suspected creative of my family. Mom's hobbies as an actor and artist as well as her writing and editing career eclipsed all possibilities for me to measure up. Dad channeled ingenuity into chasing a million dollars or saving the world, sometimes both. Before I turned ten, he invented pocket sandwiches filled with barbecued beef he called Meaty Bites, an unknown precursor to Hot Pockets.

Although my oldest sister Kathleen acted and directed stage productions, she also wrote and published some of her work in various magazines. So, I dubbed her the writer. Kristine also acted and sang jingles she composed. I called her the actor. Yvonne painted landscapes with watercolors, including the one hanging in my writing room. She also created sculptures illustrating her fine arts degree. I labeled her the artist. I remember Steven's desk strewn with electrical items and a soldering iron during his teens. He taught me how to multiply with a slide rule. He often managed the lighting and other effects from backstage when Mom performed in or directed plays. I considered Steven as creative in a techie way. Quintin mimed and moved as an automaton robot so well a store showcased him as their novelty mannequin. He also won a poetry award in high school. He taught me how to dance. I idolized his many talents. Abundant evidence supported my internal dialog when I claimed everyone but me was creative in my talented family.

My imagination extended only as far as encouraging others to develop their passions. I never dreamed I had creativity and inspiration, too. But passion waited for me in the shadows where I had buried it after my terrifying ordeal with Phil. Dormant almost five decades, eventually despair dug into me so deeply, it compelled me to write. I now appreciate how, like salt raising the sweetness of sugar in baking, anguish raised creative inspiration.

After publishing poems, books, and blogs, as well as composing songs and ongoing writing projects, I suppose I can't assert barren creativity anymore. I am artistic with a flourishing passion. They intertwine. I don't always know what I'll say, but somehow a message finds its voice now.

CR&SO

In Mom's final years, when she said she had done everything she wanted and was ready to "go boom," I believed her. Now, I'm second-guessing. I wonder if she limited herself to pursue only her most realistic dreams. Could she have stifled her passions, without realizing it, the way she repressed emotions?

Mom worked at the university's motion picture studio, set up by a former Disney animator. Hired as a secretary, her way with words, dramatic flair, and interest in the arts evolved into story editor and production supervisor positions until she retired early, in her mid-fifties.

I was a teenager when Mom left the film studio. Dad locally mass-produced the pocket sandwiches he had been perfecting. But his fledgling business soon went bust, and she returned to the workforce. She first joined a children's magazine, later edited and typeset books for a small publisher, and finally wrote and edited at a children's music company. After a few years, she retired again. She intended to create her own book publishing business and resume drawing and painting.

However, several months into her second retirement, money challenges struck again. From the time she left, the music company had been asking Mom to reconsider. Eventually, her desire for stability crushed entrepreneurship and artistic leisure. Her expected free time disappeared. She remained full time at the children's music company several more years, until a third and final retirement in her early seventies.

I read that eighty percent of adults in the USA dream of authoring a book, but only three percent of writers finish their novels. (Epstein 2002) (Zink 2017) Despite impaired vision, Dad spent his last four years laboring over a manuscript. His original motivation was to get rich from selling the books while converting the world to his religious beliefs. After medication moderated his mania, the moneymaking allure faded, and his focus shifted to spreading the love of his faith. By using a magnifying lens, he revised countless drafts but did not secure permission for the many copyrighted images he included. Only his children received a copy, the final testimony of his faith.

I wonder if Mom also held an unacknowledged desire to write and publish a book. She wrote and edited volumes of

The Light Within

scripts and manuscripts not only for the film studio and book publisher but also for freelance clients. Except for one magazine article, the stories she edited and produced were not *her* stories.

She spent free time in her sixties and seventies performing in community theater, film, and television. She never made it to Hollywood, but top studios filmed in our city. Initially, she played as an extra in major productions. Later, agents cast her in speaking roles, qualifying her to join the Screen Actors Guild, a coveted rite of passage for professional actors.

As teens, Quintin and I joined Mom as extras in *Take Down*, starring Lorenzo Lamas. With Quintin's model six foot, two inch physique, blue-green eyes, and wavy, dark-brown hair, the crew selected him as Lamas's stand-in. I was excited Quintin acted as a handsome substitute until I realized he wouldn't appear onscreen. However, Mom set herself apart from the background crowd. During a routine scene, she wielded a comic performance and landed a billing in the movie credits.

On the surface, it would appear Mom's children, career, theatrical performances, and artwork all gave her complete satisfaction. The notion of an unexpressed desire to author a book and tell her own stories still nags at me, though.

I want to test my theory, so I tilt back in my writing chair, prop my feet on a stool, quiet my mind, and ease into a meditative moment.

Today, Mom sparkles in her favorite pantsuit. Cherry lipstick matches her outfit. To me, red represents passion.

We sit shoulder to shoulder on the cuddle chair's comfy cushioning. Our fingers interlace, and I slip into her gentle and embracing love.

"Do you still believe you've done everything you ever wanted to do?"

She considers how she was blessed with six lovely children.

They filled her heart and were her number one priority. She was fortunate because life guided her through artistry. As a teen, a magazine published her drawings. Decades of theater and movie performances allowed creative expression. All those seemed enough for her. To ask much more of the Lord would have appeared ungrateful. In conclusion, she says, "Well, I felt pretty fulfilled . . . and lucky, but I suppose the answer is no."

We recount how practice enhanced her natural flair for editing and writing skills. She excelled and received compliments about her cleverness, although inadequacy bothered her. Criticism played in her head, remnants from her father's scolding in childhood and a striving to make things perfect. Insecurities waited to unravel in adulthood. A tremendous career evolved for her during a period when a woman shouldn't act out those kinds of ambitions.

Mom relegated acting to hobby status. Similarly, writing or editing required a mainstream job in a company. Freelance work ran in parallel. The few times she dared to expand her creative career horizons, money issues jolted her back to a job's steady paycheck. Pragmatism built a fence around higher aspirations.

I zero in on one last question. "If you thought you could've succeeded and fulfilled your passions—really let them loose—would you have done it?"

"Oh, boy. You know, no one can change the past. But, yeah. I would have chased bigger dreams."

Mom describes an alternative version where more would unfold without her planning every practical aspect. In this scenario, she would surrender to divine inspiration without prematurely halting her dreams. Authoring a book stands at the top of her list.

She smiles at me. "I'm proud of you for uncovering your passions and starting to pursue them."

I flash a smile in return and recall how, most of my life, I didn't acknowledge my passions. Although I dismissed its importance, the absence eventually caused me to question how I fit in the world or what else gave me meaning besides family. But I just say, "Thanks."

My fingers stop typing. I open my eyes and rest my chin on my palm. This conversation about *her* passions makes me wonder if there's anything about *my* passions I might still be overlooking.

I tuck that thought away for later. Another idea catches my attention, anyway.

13 FINDING FRANCES

Four generations of women . . .

MY MIDDLE NAME is Frances. I disliked it even though it's Mom's middle name, too.

As children, Quintin and I sometimes sang our names backward. Elizabeth Frances turned into "Theb-ah-zee-lee Sick-narf." I winced at the "sick" part, so whether backward or forward, saying Frances caused me to cringe.

When I grew up, I discovered Frances is also Grandma Mary's middle name. It originates in Great-Grandpa Wills's family. Fifteen years his junior, Great-Grandaunt Frances was the youngest and still a little girl when Great-Grandpa Wills left their farm in the late 1870s. I suppose he wanted to draw his baby sister nearer as a cherished namesake. Eventually, his other brothers and sisters also emigrated to the USA, leaving Frances alone with their widowed mother.

Shortly after Grandma Mary was born, Great-Grandpa Wills had saved enough money to send for his mother and Aunt Frances to visit. They crossed the Atlantic sea by ship and stopped in Pennsylvania to reconnect with Great-Grandpa Wills's siblings living there.

While in the East, Great-Grandpa Wills's brothers and sisters filled their mother and Aunt Frances with tall tales of

Utah and the untamed West. They voiced concern someone might force nineteen-year-old Frances into a plural marriage.

The pair ventured no farther than Pennsylvania before sailing back to Ireland. About twelve years later, in his forties, Great-Grandpa Wills's church called him to a two-year mission in his homeland. But by that time, his mother had long since died. (Simmerman 1980)

It breaks my heart that after Great-Grandpa Wills moved to the USA, he never saw his mother again. I console myself with this idea: his initial tribute to his sister Frances has now linked four generations of women in the USA to his Irish roots through our shared middle name.

I contemplate how I joined two nicknames from different stages of my life—"Beth" and "Liz"—into "Elizabeth" while writing *From the Shadows* and how healing that was. Perhaps something about my middle name, Frances, beckons me to explore as well. The idea stirs something within and beyond me. *Could it be a loving story of lineage spreading across the sea and into the unknown?* Even though I've never seen a picture of her, inspiration urges me to seek Great-Grandaunt Frances.

I swivel in my writing chair and return my fingertips to the keyboard. I shut my eyes, take three slow breaths, and ease into the cuddle chair.

Frances appears with chestnut-brown hair hanging thick and straight, beyond her shoulders. Her soft eyes mix shades of green and brown with gold flecks. Her upper lip makes a slender line over a plump lower lip, like Grandma's. The way her eyes pleat down a faint outer slant with her eyelids sweeping to a modest arch look similar to my aunt Gwen and me. At first, I think it's funny how she combines features from several women in the family, but I correct myself. We carry traits resembling Aunt Frances.

The Light Within

Her Irish lilt soothes me with its lullaby rhythm. "May this guiding light allow you to shine from within the way 'twas meant to be: purpose, passion, and meaning, blazing bright a path for others. Let a fire within kindle amor—an encompassing love of yourself, expanding and extending to all."

When she switches to a vignette from her life, I realize much more than a name connects us.

14 TWEEDED TORMENTOR

Her head buzzes like a hornet's nest . . .

ON A VERDANT knoll overlooking patchworked green and brown farmland, young Frances wears a tan play dress. A matching pinafore drapes her body until just below the knees. Her hair falls past her shoulders in twin braids. Near a large oak tree, she and her friend Annie flounce their rag dolls across a stump for a stage. The sun scatters a rosy glow across their cheeks while they chit chat for their dolls.

Spring paints the hills with yellow and white daisies in every direction, mixing their fragrance with the morning's crisp mist. Giggles bounce and bound in the meadow as much as their antics.

The flowers dance in the wind and tickle her legs, so Frances puts down her doll and decides to take some blooms home. She figures they'll perk up farmhouse grays and browns with spring colors. She plucks a few florets and raises their sweet petals under her nose, almost kissing them. Frances remembers the picked ones will die, so she decides to replant a bunch with their roots intact.

She and Annie search under the oak for sturdy twigs. They scratch the earth until they carve a trench around a clump and scoop out the moist soil. Intent on their digging, they don't notice the newcomer until a shadow looms.

As their irises adjust, they recognize the man from town. Frances regards his russet hair and matching handlebar mustache. He wears a medium-brown tweed waistcoat and acts polished. He asks questions about their dolls and digging. Everything appears polite on the surface, but something about the way he blathers sends a subtle shudder through Frances.

Annie makes excuses about the time, blurting something about her ma expecting her, and scoots down the hill with both dolls. Frances considers Annie impolite, leaving their visitor. However, Frances searches for a pretext, too. Her mind scurries alongside Annie, but her bare feet root to the spot while her tongue twists in silence. A gnawing in her gut growls at her to scamper away, but the man asks Frances all kinds of questions, and she can't figure out how to end the conversation.

He settles on the stump and invites her closer to examine the bouquet she clutches. Standing near him weakens her knees and squeezes her chest. He pats his leg for her to sit.

Even at eight, she realizes manners dictate she should show respect for elders. So, she obliges. His bony leg pokes into her thigh. When his long fingers claim their grip on her knee, her head buzzes like a hornet's nest ready to fly. Minutes pass. He blusters blarney while she politely nods. His voice drones non-stop.

Frances reminds herself she's a proper young one, and god-fearing girls don't allow his behavior. The firm *don't* she declares in her mind refuses to form on her lips. Her heart pounds harder and thumps in her throat.

She's shoved into a standing position with her back toward him while he remains seated. Her cheeks flush and burning tears tumble after he wrenches her dress up and drawers down.

The Light Within

She squirms in vain to cover her lower half, but the grip on her arm holds as tight as a tourniquet. The daisies fall to the ground.

Words like "floozie," "never breathe a word," and "reputation in tatters" sting her ears. The hillside blossoms blur.

Her arm throbs in agony. Her entire body stiffens in fear of what may happen next, but his grip soon loosens.

Frances yanks her drawers waist-high before fleeing.

Her blossoms stay strewn on the hill.

She finds Annie perching on a rock along a bend in the road, scratching the surface with a stick. Her letters form no words. "Frances, are you all right?"

Frances nods but her bottom lip quivers.

They plod in silence to their homes.

Hours turn into days, weeks, and months. Bitterness chokes Frances when she catches glimpses of her tweeded tormentor. Grateful every time she evades another encounter alone, echoes of his threats smother any ideas to divulge.

Her desire to play among the daisies withers and wanes to naught.

15 MY MIRRORS

I blame myself...

Aunt Frances's story makes me realize ridding myself of Phil remains unfinished. I'm not sure what's next, but I've had a few days to mull over everything. I know I can't do it alone. I relax on my writing chair, close my eyes, and breathe deeply three times. As I ease into this round of visualizations, I find myself standing outside a park entrance with Mom. The overgrown bushes and ironwork form a canopied entryway. I get the idea Mom should wait there for me, lending emotional support from a distance.

I walk inside and notice an enormous elm tree to my right spreads its leafy branches over a section of the expansive grounds. In contrast to the carpet of grass covering the left side and beyond, this shaded section bares brown. The chill autumn air hangs in stillness. The absence of birds or other sounds intensifies the crunching under my feet as I tread the path. A sudden gust whips past and wakes the resting leaves. I shiver and clutch my clothes tighter. I detect a figure ahead, beyond the elm.

An elderly lady rests on a park bench, its slats a weather-beaten green. Wrought iron caps each end with rosettes and fleurs-de-lis. She clenches a charcoal-black book in her leathery hands.

I stop.

She beams at me. A threadbare shawl as black as mourning covers her head, making her eyes appear like distant blue stars twinkling. Wisps of breath float in the air as she exhales, but she's cloaked head to toe from its nip. Her long dress, laced shoes, and thick stockings match the book's hue.

Although she seems smaller than usual, and something about her face doesn't seem right, I recognize Mrs. Joren. She says nothing, but I sense she conveys a message about Phil.

Dredging up the thought of him sends icy chills snaking through my limbs. My gut knots more than Mrs. Joren's knuckles. I stiffen, twist away from her, and glance back at Mom. Water wells in my eyes, but I dam them.

Mom nods and lifts her hands as if pushing the air toward me three times in quick succession to encourage me.

Despite my reluctance, I focus on my inhales and exhales. A shift in sensation emerges. A faint warmth bubbles, giving me the impression talking to Mrs. Joren may help.

I pivot back toward Mrs. Joren and walk closer. "Please, tell me what you want to say. I'm listening."

She provides background about the shawl she crocheted and emigrating to the USA many years before. As she continues, she wants me to know Phil suffered terrible incidents and never recovered. For decades, she supposed Phil wasn't completely healthy but refused to admit it to herself.

Instead, she read sacred passages from her black book every day, hoping for insights or a miracle. She sobbed in silence when she couldn't pinpoint what was different about her son. Desperate to rescue Phil, she despaired in how. So, most of the time, she banished her disturbing hunches into a stygian hollow.

Her eyes downcast, she pauses, draws in a heavy breath,

and pours out what she's bottled up for decades. She finishes by saying, "I blame myself . . . what happened to you."

She wails as teary waterfalls cover her olive complexion before buffeting her chest.

My eyes mist while she loses all composure.

I barely make out what she blubbers next. "I left you alone with him. Why I didn't take you to da door?"

She becomes somewhat coherent as she describes what she witnessed: me dashing down the stairs, scooting past her, and sprinting out the front door. She intended to confront Phil, but she cowered. If she didn't ask, she could still pretend it wasn't true.

Soon afterward, she fell ill and didn't have the strength to do anything about it before she died.

I lay a hand on her left shoulder and slide it down to rub her back. "I never blamed you." I pat my face dry and give Mrs. Joren time to collect herself, too.

When her attention returns to the present, she looks up at me, and her face brightens again. "I give a gift but need your help. I love you like a granddaughter. Can we hug and remember da good times?"

I adore Mrs. Joren. It's a major reason Beth feels so betrayed by Phil. She trusted him as much as Mrs. Joren. "Sure, but it's not me who needs to. It's Beth."

I call Beth onto the scene and have her stand on my left. Beneath her purple and white-polka-dot dress, she's still missing her underwear.

Mrs. Joren looks toward her. "So sorry, Beth. You did nothing wrong. Phil did something bad because he was sick. I didn't know how to help him then, but I know how to help you now."

She sets the black book aside and offers outstretched arms. Beth plops on the bench and slides into a cozy clasp, burrowing her cheek in Mrs. Joren's soft bosom and dill scent.

Phil appears and stands about thirty feet away from the end of the bench. His dark-brown eyes seek my attention. I strain to hear him say, "I am so sorry."

My stomach churns, and I scowl.

He's still dressed in a white top and black slacks. Held only by his thumb and index finger, he waves a small, white cloth. Beth glares at Phil's hairy hands, purses her lips together, whips her head the opposite way, and pretends he's invisible.

His peace offering takes shape: Beth's panties.

Phil studies me. "I *am* sorry. I beg your forgiveness." He tells me how it would mean a lot and how he thinks forgiveness would help us both. He realizes what he did was shocking and hurtful. Most of all, he understands how he betrayed my trust. He regrets how I lost my passion for writing and buried it because of him. "I'm so sorry for what I did . . . how it hurt you. Please accept my deepest apology."

I sigh and point. "Forgiveness falls to Beth."

Mrs. Joren strokes a few wisps of hair away from Beth's forehead.

Beth's still not looking at Phil, so I ask her what she wants to do. She doesn't dare go anywhere near him. Instead, she climbs sideways onto Mrs. Joren's lap, keeping her back toward Phil. Mrs. Joren gently rocks her while humming a lullaby. Beth rests her eyes and nestles her head against Mrs. Joren.

Many minutes pass before Beth leaps up, snatches her panties from Phil, and darts behind the elm's protective trunk. She steps her foot inside one opening then the other and adjusts her undies beneath the dress.

Beth marches back to the bench. She stands straight with

her chest puffed out and, to my surprise, takes command. "Okay. Here's what we'll try. Mrs. Joren, hug me. Phil can hug you at the same time, but he's not allowed to touch me." Beth scoots onto Mrs. Joren's lap, faces forward, and shuts her eyes tight.

Mrs. Joren wraps her arms around Beth.

Phil makes his way to the back of the bench, behind her and Mrs. Joren. When Beth hears leaves crunch under his feet, her back stiffens and hands curl into fists.

Phil hunches over and overlaps his mother's arms with his own. While they extend their hugs, Phil stays careful not to brush against Beth. This way, each recognizes the other's presence, and Phil can express his penitence while Mrs. Joren shields Beth.

He whispers, "I'm so sorry. I have profound regret. I acted deranged. Please allow me to apologize for my betrayal and again say how truly and deeply sorry I am for everything. You were a wonderful little girl. I picked you because of how sweet you were. It made me suppose your sweetness might somehow rub off and cure me. A weird and twisted thought, for sure, but that was my rationale. Beth, please forgive me."

I watch minutes pass as Beth's face softens, her hands uncurl, and she leans her back against Mrs. Joren's bosom. When she finally opens her eyes, she releases a protracted sigh and turns toward him. She surprises me with her maturity.

"Phil, I forgive you." She motions for him to come around to the front. "Close your eyes. I'll show you my heart and the spirit of love it carries."

Phil closes his eyes.

"And, Phil, show me yours, too. Show me your heart and the caring spirit within you."

Beth closes her eyes.

I watch them during the next few minutes. Electricity courses throughout the air and within my body in a way so profound words cannot explain.

Beth slides off Mrs. Joren's lap and sits next to her. Beth looks up at Phil. "I can give you a real hug now." He stoops and brings Beth in his arms. She responds in kind.

As they embrace, their bodies tremble. All their pent-up anguish pierces the chill air in heart-wrenching weeping.

Eventually, both release all their grieving as the sun weaves ribbons of light. The warming atmosphere sends soothing vibrations through all of us.

Beth releases her grasp and so does Phil. She says, "This time, let's try something different. Here, sit on the bench. We can make it as wide as we want."

The seat stretches four more feet to accommodate the three of them. Beth gestures for Phil to lie on the seat and cradles his head in her lap.

Beth's voice softens to a whisper. "I feel like God's here, helping us both to heal." She searches his warm, brown eyes. "Phil Joren, I forgive you for everything you did to me."

She strokes his raven-black hair and raises his head from her lap. She asks Phil to kneel on the ground, so they meet at eye level when she stands. Beth pecks Phil's cheek. "I send you on your way. I cut the tie binding us."

Beth hands one half of Mrs. Joren's black shawl to Phil and me while she and Mrs. Joren take the other half. We unravel our respective corners until the last strands come undone in the middle, and the lace becomes a loose pile of thread.

"I set *you* free.

"I set *me* free.

"I set *we* free."

The Light Within

This time, neither sheds a tear in their tight embrace. Beth and Phil clasp each other in a vibrant glow. After exchanging farewell words with Beth and me, Phil strolls away. His image fades with the horizon's shimmer.

I glance at Mrs. Joren. She arranges something white. During the time we exchanged goodbyes, she crocheted the finishing touches on a delicate lace shawl. She places it over her head. "I am the Source of all. I am no longer Mrs. Joren but a messenger of spirit speaking through her. You have been courageous. You will receive true healing."

Mrs. Joren's dress turns cloudy white, and she exudes radiance. She's a beautiful, young woman and becomes younger and younger until she transforms into a little girl with raven locks cascading to her waist.

Her image merges with Beth, and I reabsorb Beth. I realize we are all connected. Phil Joren represents a part of myself, a lingering shame and distrust overshadowing my choices and tormenting me. Mrs. Joren also symbolizes a side of me. Although the circumstances differ, the emotion is the same: she's a mirror for my mom guilt, and he reflects my darkest deeds.

I now stand bathed by the white shawl as Elizabeth Frances. I glisten, luminous with an alternating opaque and transparent shine. I imagine I could fly straight to the sky as a shooting star and blend with all that is. I am part of the universe.

I head to the entryway and rejoin Mom. We discuss this scene. I'm perplexed why Mrs. Joren's eyes shone blue instead of brown. Mom's mouth curves upward, and eyes gleam knowingly. A surging realization spreads over me. I substituted Mrs. Joren's eyes with Mom's familiar blue twinkles.

"Thanks, Mom, for being a part of the reconciliation. I realize in forgiving them, I also begin forgiving myself."

JUGGLING JUDGMENTS

When I make one mistake, I obsess about other issues, and rush to the conclusion I'm not good enough

16 COMPASSIONATE COMPOSITIONS

Empathic listening clarifies without needing to agree . . .

SEEKING FRANCES AND forgiving Phil completes a capstone, but letting go isn't just about big stressors. Lasting inner harmony requires regular practice about smaller ones, too.

I recall several years ago, my emotions bounced between worthlessness and hopelessness. When they replayed in my mind, I worried they would never leave.

Then, I read about the drama triangle and compassion triangle in Dr. Karpman's book, *A Game Free Life*. (Karpman 2014) Three dysfunctional characters make up the drama triangle: a rescuer, a victim, and a persecutor. Some models also call them a hero, a victim, and a villain. The essence is the same. The drama escalates as roles change. I can play all three alone or with others.

As it applies to negative self-talk, the drama triangle's persecutor punishes, the rescuer protects, and the victim pities.

Depression propels the persecutor to the forefront, an inner critic preying on foibles and sucking out joy. Alone, my despair would berate my every failure and pound out scores of chiding internal chatter, insisting what a horrible mother I had been.

It took years to deal with the toxic self-talk as I healed from depression. Although I didn't fantasize about killing myself anymore, guilt and shame lurked as terrible triangle playmates. When I thought of Phil, I would feel sorry for myself (victim). *Why me? Why him? Why that?*

Or, I would chastise myself (persecutor) for being so stupid. *You should've left after baking. You shouldn't have gone upstairs with him. You should've said no.*

And, I would try to defend my actions and inactions (rescuer). *How would I have known better, at six? How could I have predicted what he did?*

Cycles of negative self-talk would repeat. Not dealing with my shame helped me stay a victim. Even though it was painful, victimization rewarded me with a payoff. I could remain powerless, wallowing in self-pity. I could get sympathy or attention from others. As a victim, I didn't have to put forth any effort to change or fix myself. I could keep blaming Phil. And, I could continue beating up on myself about my motherhood failures. As opposed to the unknowns involved in change, the unpleasant sameness produced a sense of familiar certainty. I call this a "comfortable discomfort."

I imagined facing the issue head-on would cause even more distress and effort. The idea I would step outside my well-known but torturing drama triangle frightened me. I had played its game for so long, I needed practice avoiding the persecutor, victim, and rescuer roles. One part would dominate more than the other two, but I played all three in dysfunction. And, as I flipped from one role to another, it intensified cruel self-talk.

I did something about destructive dialog by noticing when I was trapped in its vicious cycle. At first, I viewed interactions in retrospect. Eventually, I analyzed them in real time. Finally, I stepped out of the triangle's snare when drama was underway or sometimes avoided stumbling into it altogether.

When I played this terrible game with others, there were a few ways to end the drama. One means was through an apology. By expressing regret at any point, we stopped the argument from escalating. "Sorry, I misunderstood." A second approach voiced appreciation. "Thanks for the reminder," instead of saying, "I know, I know, do you think I'm stupid?" A third tactic used empathic listening which rephrased the content and named the underlying emotion.

Empathic listening underpins Dr. Covey's fifth habit. (Covey 2004) He calls it "seek first to understand, then to be understood." I appreciate how empathic listening clarifies without needing to agree. The technique also offers crucial calm during heated arguments. Unfortunately, I need it most when I'm least inclined to use it. When I'm upset or strongly disagree, I usually want to prove I'm right. Striving for perfection propels my need to be right.

The compassion triangle also has persecutor, rescuer, and victim, but they are positive versions of each. A positive persecutor supplies determination, power, and purpose. A positive rescuer offers love, healing, and protection. A positive victim embraces acceptance, vulnerability, and growth.

Dr. Karpman suggests a "ten percent solution." The compassion triangle presumes whatever roles people play, they act with some positive motivation or intention. Regardless of what we perceive, any triangular game includes at least a ten percent mix of positive intention, truthfulness, untruthfulness, commonality, and simultaneous role-playing. (Karpman 2014)

For example, I was facilitating a leadership training in Ethiopia a few years ago. At the close of the first day, I gathered participants in a circle and asked them to identify a key takeaway or insight from our discussions. One participant said he thought I should be able to speak more Amharic after so many visits. I bristled. *He's making me look bad.* (victim) *I asked for insights, not feedback about me.* (rescuer) My persecutor wanted to fight back and tell the guy he was wrong. "You didn't follow the instructions. I was asking for insights about the content." Instead, I managed to say, "Thank you for your feedback," and moved on to the next person.

In my hotel room that night, the participant's comment played over and over within my inner drama triangle. *I don't live in Ethiopia. I say lots of Amharic phrases but by the time I come back, I've forgotten some of what I've learned* (rescuer). *What a rude thing to say in front of everyone.* (persecutor). As I examined my thoughts and feelings about the incident, I had a flash of insight. I decided the next day I would clarify what his intent was and use it as an example in the class. After all, one of our topics was communication.

The next morning, I asked the participant for more context to understand his comment about wanting me to speak better Amharic. He explained he'd worked with another foreigner who quickly learned Amharic. As he told the story, I realized he wasn't trying to embarrass me. He held me in high regard and wanted a greater sense of connection he thought could come from us speaking the same language. I walked the class through this interaction as an example of how difficult it is to know someone's intent.

The drama triangle makes assumptions, but the compassion triangle clarifies context.

My current focus for forgiving myself entails mastering the compassion triangle on a routine basis, so I can apply it during crucial moments for both myself and others.

Meantime, I'm getting better at noticing not just my thoughts but also my body's signals about whether I'm in the drama triangle or the compassion triangle.

17 FACING FEAR

Fear can propel, but I allow it to paralyze . . .

MONTHS LATER, I wake with a jolt. A heaviness crushes my chest. My heart's racing and sweat beads along my hairline. Usually, I would roll over and try to shake it off by going back to sleep. Instead, I get up and do something about it. I force myself out of bed and lumber to my writing room.

Is it anxiety? Something else? Whatever the sensation, this must be a drama triangle of my making.

In my writing chair, I close my eyes. I manage only shallow inhales and exhales, but inspiration still seeps through.

I picture the three globes from before: white to my left, obsidian to my right, and the blend in front of me. Still, I can't trace the source.

Mom. I need Mom's guidance. My breaths deepen only slightly and fingers ready as I retreat to the cuddle chair.

A white-flowered necklace rings her collarbone. I scoot beside her and caress her hand. I start my ritual and stroke her almost transparent skin. Bluish veins raise rivers below and across her wrist. Straight ridges form at her cuticle and end at the tips. I compare them to ridges on my nails and wonder what causes the striations. Her platinum diamond ring and gold band slide loose on her finger.

Outside the parlor, the sun's rays yawn just above the horizon, ready to release golden streaks across the brightening blue sky.

"You worry more than you need to." She also tells me to examine the source of my concerns before the rising tightness in my chest engulfs me.

I follow her instructions and hold the fear ball with both hands, noting its full weight.

"Describe every sensation. Tell me how your body feels and whatever thoughts jumble around."

I heft this midnight-with-no-moon globe and grapple with its force as it rotates inside.

"My chest constricts. Knots kink from my stomach upward to my breast. I can't catch my breath."

We talk about all the thoughts churning in my mind, too.

Yesterday, one week's worth of work got wiped out by a corrupted hard drive. My consulting client has been waiting for an update. This delay will disappoint them. *Why me?* I try to remind myself that's my victim talking. My inner critic pesters me again. *You screwed up. You didn't back up your work. Stupid.* Maybe I am dumb, since here's clear evidence. But I don't want to look stupid. That's the issue.

"Why do you worry about looking stupid?"

"I don't want to fail. When I make one mistake, I obsess about other issues, and rush to the conclusion I'm not good enough."

It's the perfectionist in me. One flaw spills over into every flaw possible, real or imagined. "But it's basic, isn't it? Everyone feels inadequate in some way or worries they're lacking."

"Yes, but what are *your* connections to imperfection? What else could you consider?"

"Well, *you* were practically perfect in every way. That's a high threshold right there."

I chuckle and wink. "But I already know that. I suppose I should search further."

"Peer into the globe. Look at your reflection and all negative distortions. Sweetie, face your worries by chatting with fear."

I've faced fears before but not by directly talking to them. I wait to catch my breath while my heart pounds in my throat.

"Hi, fear. How are you today?"

I can't see any features.

"You transfix yourself, and I guzzle your stagnant sweat," it says.

Yuck. My body shivers.

"Okay, well, thanks for being honest. How can I push through rather than remain paralyzed?"

"Hmm. That's something you need to figure out for yourself. Everybody has different triggers."

"But you're my own special fear, aren't you?"

"No." The "o" echoes in a snicker. "You're not unique. Everyone's this way. This is universal. I'm not discriminatory. Some people deny me until I make them burst in anxiety, but others confront me as you're doing now. Everybody has degrees of dread. Your terror about not being good enough tastes delectable."

I shiver again. *God, what is this monster?* "Mom, it enjoys my misery and worry."

In one graceful motion, Mom strokes my jawline with her index finger, pushes my hair back, and tucks strands behind my ear.

Her voice sounds as gentle as her touch. "I love you just as you are. You know this, already, but I'm reminding you." She explains how when worries dominate my thoughts and I beat up on myself, I stay in the drama triangle. Apprehension and anxiety block me from what I most desire. She explains a new concept to me: fear can propel, but I allow it to paralyze.

She encourages me to leverage the opposites in partnership. Love and fear serve as a dyad. Fear encourages discernment. Love promotes comfort and flow, but a brook needs direction. Fear steadies my path, so the banks don't overflow, flood, or wander willy-nilly. I should channel my energy with productive fear and embrace love's speed and smoothness. "Does that make sense to you?"

"So, worries can operate as a rudder. Whereas love accepts everything the way it is, positive fear enables me to steer clear of barriers."

"Well, you can interpret a variety of ways, but your version sounds just fine."

Mom explains how when I yield to negativity, it's akin to getting stuck in a sandbar or paddling in circles. All part of my awareness, I should allow myself to experience the fear yet progress through it. Explore the reason. Wonder about my physical sensations and emotional connections. I can clear mental murkiness by plunging into my past to alter my future.

Blockage and flow form a fluid cycle. When I transcend constraints, they convert into love. As I constrict love, it logjams into fear.

She encourages me to enjoy both smooth sailing and whitewater rapids. "Life's flux will never be more difficult than you can handle, whether you pass through or around them. Look beyond the surface."

I reexamine the globe and dive deeper.

Beyond losing the data, beyond being perfect. What's the connection?

I'm in uncharted territory. I've started a writing career, but I don't dare phase out my consulting work yet.

Why? Money? Yeah, but only partly. Not the whole reason. What then?

It's beyond the data crashing.

Consulting serves as my safety net. I'm good at it. Screwing up the work threatens my security. But that also reminds me, I'm making mistakes in other ways.

My jaw clenches and body shudders in a chain reaction.

Maybe I'm not good enough to be a full-time writer.

Shit.

Gotta try looking at this another way.

Right. I'm new to writing.

What if . . . it's reasonable to make mistakes when I start something new?

I set the obsidian ball aside as my mind searches for a time when I considered mistakes a normal part of life. I recall as a kid when I learned how to ride a bike. I fell and skinned my knees. That didn't stop me. That didn't make me stupid.

My toes barely pushed down the pedals as I straddled a big-boy bike. I remember my ninth Christmas. A girl's purple Schwinn Stingray with a white banana seat and cruiser handlebars waited in the living room. I rode outside in the freezing snow until slush soaked my dress. I ran inside, changed, and rode again.

Eventually, riding became effortless. By summer, I could tuck a friend behind me and squeeze another between the handlebars. Alone, I pedaled until I mastered stretches of hands-free riding.

Perhaps life is similar. Practice balancing between the left, right, and forward motion until a second nature kicks in, and I barely need to steer.

I'm still learning to ride this new, creative writing career and skinning mental knees. So, keeping the long term in mind, why not remind myself I've fallen before and succeeded. Ultimately, inexperience turns into effortless abilities. Balancing along my new path just takes practice.

I open my eyes. From my writing chair, I remember my earlier visit with Mom about not fulfilling her passions. It dawns on me what I overlooked about fulfilling mine.

18 FLOWING FORMATIONS

Explore inner landscapes . . .

As I step into soft sand at the shoreline's cusp, cresting white waves glide toward my feet. I clasp Beth's hand. I place my hands around her waist, pick her up as high as I can, and twirl her around. We giggle and hoot.

The breeze caresses while the waves crest. The sun ends its radiance as it descends toward the horizon. Seagulls call overhead. I watch their V formation shift to a U pattern before they form the V again. Their ebb and flow follow rhythms. *Should I absorb and adapt? Drift back and forth as the tide? Ebb and flow, like the birds flocking in and out of the formation, winging onward?*

Ebbs provide opportunities to explore inner landscapes.

Through our deep dives, emotions Beth and I had submerged for decades rise freely in effervescence. Their sensations invigorate. Their power blesses us and transcends our individual bodies. In the sharing, we connect in powerful ways to heal. We embrace a simple interchange of pure love between our individual spirit and the Divine.

I shift my imagination from the beach to the cuddle chair. Weeks have passed since our last conversation.

"Mom, what's next?"

"You're not ready."

"What? Not ready?" Guess I should follow my own advice. I wrote a practice where I say you might not accept what your beloved says, and you might show resistance. Maybe I'm not as receptive as I could be.

"Do I need to try something else first?"

"Yes."

"Can you give me guidance?"

She chuckles. "Of course. Write out your worst fear. Say both what and why."

That's not what I want to do, but I trust her advice.

What is my worst fear?

I agonize a lot about my writing. Beyond my doubts about being able to make it my career, I worry sharing my experiences won't help anybody. *But is my writing the worst fear?* I draw in a deep breath, and the thought evaporates. That concern doesn't jar me enough to be the worst.

My mind whizzes as I wonder about other issues, but none of them prompt me to cry. Crying signals when I've struck a nerve, either profound joy or unrecognized pain. I clenched my teeth, mentioning the last notion. This must embody pain I need to heal. I suffer fewer, less severe headaches. I still ache in my back and shoulders. I believe these physical issues are connected to emotional remnants I'm working through—ongoing release.

What terror do I avoid?

My breathing shallows and belly tightens. I hug my sides and coil into a knot after a follow-up sucker punch.

The Light Within

Bingo.
My children will reject me.

I consciously know my kids love me. We've spoken about some of my failures as a mother—not that *I am* a failure, but *I have had* failures. I've hurt them through my actions and inactions. Since they've already forgiven me about so many issues, why this unrelenting anxiety?

My recent experience with Phil helps me appreciate forgiveness isn't just for the other person. It heals me, too. When I forgive someone else or express remorse, I release emotional toxins.

But what connection about forgiveness and rejection should I explore now?

I embrace the thought of ebbing and flowing emotions until my aha moment: carryover from last night's squabble with Gillis about our adult kids left me edgy.

Decades-old regrets make me cringe even during recent issues. I believe I should have done something differently about how we corrected them as children. I preferred to punish by grounding or temporarily taking away a privilege. Gillis deemed my tactics either too lenient or drawn-out deprivation. Sure, I swatted our kids' behinds sometimes, but I wasn't comfortable being the primary disciplinarian, so I saddled him with it.

When difficult scenes from the past popped in my mind, I blamed him for his handling and felt ashamed I hadn't done anything right. Now, I'm noticing the perpetual loop I've created by blaming him and shaming myself—a kind of hangman's necklace when we quarrel about our kids.

I begin to realize I need to take another route. Victoria, Kenneth, and Christopher are adults now and are capable of dealing with any upbringing issues. I should focus on *my* unresolved anguish.

After all, I nurture the power to forgive myself. But Mom's right. I'm not ready yet. I still need moral support to channel an emotional ebb and flow about my mothering and to cut loose shame's stranglehold.

19 DANCE AMONG DAISIES

Renewal's gift . . .

THE NEXT MORNING, I slide into my writing chair, gently fill my lungs and exhale, and wait for Mom. But this time, we don't sit in the cuddle chair.

Before we tackle my greatest dread, she guides me from the parlor to the front entry. When she opens the door, an expansive field of yellow and white daisies ripples before me. As we enter the scene, Mom shuts the door behind us, and the house disappears.

Along my right side, a brook babbles as it continues down the hill. I note the riverbed's muted grays, browns, and tans beneath the water's surface. It crests white foam as it curves and slides down the sloping hill.

A few large boulders dot the gentle banks. The breeze welcomes my skin as refreshing morning mist blankets me in a silken caress.

Mom guides me to two rocks whose smooth surfaces curve into near-perfect chairs. Seated, she points to the hilltop, at a series of smaller trees dotting the landscape and one massive oak beyond. This beautiful scene overlooks a town.

"Aunt Frances was born and raised in that village. This is Daisy Hill, where it happened."

My mouth drops open.

"The story is true," she says.

I shiver. My whole body quivers. I exhale in staccato.

Mom tells me that the man abused many young girls around here. Nobody said a word, but people sensed something odd about him. The girls never accused him because of his power and influence. His attacks became bolder.

A sharp shudder spasms down my legs.

We continue by talking about how sexual abuse leaves its survivors with terrible wounds, no matter the degree of violence. But my thoughts replay *the story is true*. I wonder how to explain what I can't easily confirm. Besides, why should I play a role by writing about Frances?

Mom carries on as if I already voiced my question. "Trust in the Lord." She takes my hands in hers and explains that I'm recounting Aunt Frances's story because I experienced similar trauma. And, I'm already healing from my ordeal. As children, Aunt Frances and I each suffered in silent shame. Entangled decade after decade, I now unravel suppression's hold on me.

"Allow. Allow everything to release," Mom says. "You'll find appropriate words for inspiration and healing. Share insights as they arise."

She turns my attention to the brook.

"Do you hear its sounds? It purls a calming message. Invite its invigorating energy to flow through you and relieve your worries. Sense its soothing power coursing through every part of your body."

She lets go of my hands. A vibration pulses through me. Warm tingles usher a peaceful release from my crown to my soles.

The daisies wriggle in waves across the hill. I inhale their fresh-rain scent. The enormous oak tree shares its shade with surrounding vegetation and sprinkles splotches of sunshine. I throw out my arms and twirl. My dress flares until I'm dizzy and collapse on the ground giggling.

The daisies offer renewal's gift. I stoop and cup my hands around several, allowing their petals to stroke my cheeks. I bless their golden disks as if they're each my sunshine center.

Mom rests her hand on my shoulder. "Anytime you sense the need, return to these healing waters and dance among the daisies."

20 PARENTAL PROPAGANDIZER

I believed I betrayed my children . . .

LIFTED BUOYANT BY Mom's recent field trip, I'm more prepared to expose the roots and divulge my vicious inner voice, the propagandizer. During my darkest hours, mine told me I was worthless, and everyone—especially Gillis, Victoria, Kenneth, and Christopher—would be better off without me.

We all can harbor suffocating untruths we accept about ourselves. My propagandizer bombarded me many, many times about how I had failed my children.

I tried to rebuff those negative thoughts, but the harder I shoved them aside, the fiercer they burrowed.

Incidents of injuries and inattention haunted me. For example, a child clobbered three-year-old Kenneth with a sand-encrusted brick at daycare. Gillis rushed Kenneth to the doctor, and Kenneth wore an eye patch for a week. One evening I forgot it was my turn to collect the kids from daycare. I realized my mistake when one of the staff called at closing time, wondering where I was. Thankfully, the woman stayed with the kids instead of calling child protective services on me. But these are not the worst events.

Three scenes offer a glimpse into my most tainted terrain.

༄

The evening news headline grabs my attention once I hear Jerri's name. The screen's banner freezes me on the spot: "manslaughter." I process a fraction of what the newscaster reports, but "shaking, abuse, and infant death" clang alarm bells in my throat and chest.

My stare tunnels through the TV and peers into the past.

I recall Victoria's nine-month-old body fastened snug and secure in her fuzzy blue car seat but quivering. Her shuddered sobs suck out her breath while tears streak her plump olive cheeks. Her fingers clutch the crackers I offer for consolation. I hope her agitation will subside soon, but she whimpers throughout dinner. I can't figure out what's wrong, so, I excuse her behavior as a colicky phase. But day after day poses the same struggles.

A single mother in her mid-thirties, Jerri stands petite with frosted brown hair feathered short and styled in a wedged swoosh. After school, Jerri's daughters also tend the children she cares for in her home. With Victoria's spiral curls and cherubic rosy lips, Jerri's girls cuddle, carry her around, and dote on her. Their house remains clean and orderly. Gillis and I check how much formula and food remain in Victoria's bag each day. The family seems nice.

To assuage recent concerns, we've been stopping by Jerri's at unexpected times but observe nothing awry. Weeks pass without improvement. Convinced something elusive remains amiss, Gillis and I confront Jerri. We face off in her living room on opposing couches. He expresses our frustration about Victoria's persistent distress. He doesn't explicitly accuse Jerri of mistreatment but furrows his black brows, lowers his bass voice, leans forward, and braces his forearm on his thigh. "I want you to know Victoria is my only child. If anything happens to her here, I won't complain to the police."

Jerri's expression shows she grasps what he means. In response, I shift from side to side in my seat and exhale. Before he ends the conversation, Gillis lobs a couple more concerns at Jerri, but she slices the tension with sugary assurance of Victoria's safety in her care.

From then on, Victoria was happier when we picked her up. We kept a watchful eye and noticed no relapse. However, we eventually found another sitter.

Back in the present, the TV blares on about a different headline, but my mind chases unanswered questions.

When did the baby die?

Was Jerri watching Victoria then?

Did something happen to Victoria when Jerri babysat her?

I scour newspaper articles for more details and dates. The baby died several years after Victoria left Jerri's care. I read about other incidents Jerri's not charged with: using a dark closet as routine punishment, a toddler's broken leg, and a second infant's death.

Only an awful mother would confuse colic with that.

What if Gillis hadn't intervened?

Shouldn't have had to put her in daycare.

☙❧

Bawls from the basement seize my attention. I spot the downstairs door ajar. My stomach knots as I rush to rescue. Standing at the top, I spot Kenneth's six-month-old body plonked sideways in his overturned walker at the bottom.

My mind flashes through scenarios. I picture him plummeting down each of the twenty steps until he crash-lands on the concrete floor. One version has him gliding upright as the wheels bounce down each stair on his rickety ride. The other possibility rings my heart around my gut and punches so hard I grip the banister for balance. I imagine him tumbling head over heels bumping his head on stair after stair. My feet scarcely touch the steps as I rush down.

I scoop Kenneth out of the walker and dash upstairs. I clutch him to my chest, soothing his sobs. The sparse black velvet fuzz on his head makes it easy to examine. On the dining room carpet, Gillis and I press his head and search his entire body for any sign of bruising, swelling, or discomfort. No marks yet. His limbs appear intact. We study each movement of his legs, arms, fingers, and toes. Nothing seems fractured. His tears dry and chocolate-brown eyes glisten under licorice-black lashes.

I exhale and take in half a normal breath. *Maybe he'll be okay.* We monitor him for hours, making sure he suffers no concussion.

In fact, I can't find a single bruise anywhere except on my maternal ego.

Why did I leave the door open?
Why wasn't I watching him?
I'm a neglectful, horrible mother.

☙❧

Focused on building our family business, holidays interrupt the company's innumerable demands. When the kids call, I assure them we'll soon start our New Year's Eve celebrations. But time ticks by, and one last task breeds a Hydra of to-dos before I leave. Gillis promises to close the office and follow suit soon.

On my way home, I stop by the grocery store and buy noise poppers, sparkling grape juice, and other traditional treats for our midnight celebration.

I suspect something's wrong when twelve-year-old Victoria and nine-year-old Kenneth greet me tight-faced, spilling words so fast I can't process. I plop the grocery bags on the kitchen floor. Pouches filled with frozen peas and corn wrap around six-year-old Christopher's left arm and torso. Raging crimson blisters plague his skin.

Their frantic shouts sink in: To surprise us, Victoria, Kenneth, and Christopher had started our holiday tradition on their own. They mixed and rolled our customary deep-fried cookie on the kitchen table. The deep fryer spat oil as it cooked, stinging Christopher's skin. To avoid more spatters, he retreated from behind the table. But his foot caught on the electrical cord connecting the fryer to the wall outlet. Both Christopher and the fryer crashed to the tile floor. He swam in the slippery, scalding oil struggling to stand up before Victoria or Kenneth could snatch him. They rushed Christopher to the bathroom, plunged him under a cold shower to wash away the oil, and taped frozen veggie pouches to his body.

In his shock, Christopher's cocoa-colored eyes crave sleep, but the searing thwarts his rest.

My stomach hollows into a black hole, ears drone with a thousand bees, and eyes fixate on a universe of multi-colored stars. The back of my knees sting, straining to remain standing.

Gillis strides through the door, snaps me out of my daze, and urges me to rush Christopher to the emergency room.

I write the reason for our visit on the check-in sheet at the triage table. Patients fill the hospital waiting room seats, but I find one empty chair. I place Christopher on my lap and caress his short, black curls after arranging clear sandwich bags filled with ice cubes at strategic spots. I count the filled chairs trying to predict our waiting time when they call his name.

Staff show us to a private room and examine Christopher's injuries. A sleeve of charred flesh spans his left arm from the biceps to wrist. Portions of his chest ooze from golf-ball-size blisters. A nurse rolls him over and injects his bum with painkiller to numb his second- and third-degree burns, allowing him to relax and sleep. Another nurse slathers his skin with silver sulfadiazine, a white antibiotic cream for burns. When they're done dressing his entire arm in gauze and wrapping his torso, he's half a mummy.

I should have been home instead of working.
It's my fault.
I didn't protect Christopher.

～※～

For nearly thirty years, these scenes and others replayed in my mind hundreds of times. Propagandizer proclaimed me a neglectful mother and scolded I should have done more. I shouldn't work so late. I should protect them.

When in my worst bouts with depression, all those details replayed with a vengeance among my drama triangle brainchildren.

My maternal failures propagated my ultimate fear: *my children will stop loving me.*

I fought the haranguing until now. With Mom's encouragement, I wrote the worst incidents and what my propagandizer said—the *why* part. Mom advised me earlier to explore the emotion before releasing.

When shameful scenes crisscrossed my mind, I wrote my account, what I did, how I felt, and what I told myself about what happened—all the feelings and physical sensations. As I submerged in the raw emotions, they began to fade and evaporate.

Once I released each troubling memory, other memories replaced them in layers. I better grasped life's irony: I need to immerse in the same intensity of pain before I can release it and heal.

Besides writing about painful periods when I believed I betrayed my children or felt most inadequate, I discussed episodes with my family over the next several months.

Clouded perceptions about not being the perfect mother made me believe each ordeal had been my fault. By sharing various incidents with family members about what provoked my motherhood self-reproach, the air began to clear.

In some instances, I also discovered I wasn't the only one who had been shouldering self-blame for the same events. Imagine my surprise and sympathy to hear instead of condemning me, others blamed themselves, instead. The discussions helped us to begin viewing ourselves and what had happened in a gentler light.

PICKING PERSPECTIVES

As I nurture my ability to see through another's eyes, it deepens a vision of myself

21 RADIANT RESURRECTION

Reframe what we painted . . .

"How can you explain to someone still mired in the muck that they can resurrect hope and light within?" Mom asks.

"Well," I say, "In my understanding of this journey, we must heal ourselves. Because we are the ones piling up the pain. Not easy to do, but it is that simple." My attention shifts from the cuddle chair to a few years ago, when I learned about codependency.

At the time, I finally recognized how I desperately clung to other people by hinging my joy and happiness on their actions and emotions. I had tried to fix others instead of focusing on my own problems. I gave away my power and didn't feel in control of my life. After I began freeing myself of this compulsion, I penned the poem, *Changed My Life,* containing the freeing phrase "key is I'm responsible just for me." (Onyeabor 2016) Freedom from depression entails a similar key. The thoughts—the propagandizer's taunts—trick and lie to us, telling stories of inadequacy and unworthiness. Not mere figments of imagination, they pack real wallops.

However, they stem from a narrow, negative viewpoint. Several memes show how to view images from more than one perspective. One black and white drawing appears to viewers either as an old woman or a young woman. If you focus on the dark portions, an old woman with a big nose emerges from the illustration. But by focusing on the light parts, a young woman with a feather in her hat surfaces. The difference lies in perception. Our past can look ugly, *and* it can appear beautiful when we reframe what we painted.

Sometimes, we need assistance seeing beyond what conceals our beauty within. Alongside our ugly self-portrait, our most alluring image waits, ready to shine.

You may be reading this book hoping for a fantastic transformation tip I will describe.

The miracle you seek is not in me. You are the miracle.

Seize your beauty, courage, and light. You radiate beauty even if you feel unappealing. You show strength and bravery though you may judge yourself weak. You carry incredible capability even when you sink in overwhelm and exhaustion. You possess a luminous power within. Are you ready to unleash it?

You can do it. Be patient and gentle with yourself. Unwinding from your whirlpool—or however you describe your most miserable moments—takes time. However, you are capable.

When I found the path to lift my depression and reignite self-love, it was not just one way or a single book. Glean what you wish from my experience. Some reflect-and-respond activities in the back may resonate with you more than others.

Hope waits for you as an undying ember. When you resurrect the passion and purpose you forgot, or never knew you had, it will kindle a dazzling fire. So long as you fuel the blaze with passionate activities and purposeful ways, life will never dampen it again.

This message applies as much to me as to you.

I treasure newfound passion. I live it to the extent I can. The route hasn't been easy, but I find it filled with joy and excitement. I follow this new path in parallel with other daily demands. I try to prioritize my passion because it fosters delight. I continue exploring my inner terrain because my intuition advocates a routine practice of self-forgiveness and development to maintain long-lasting bliss.

So long as I live with passion and purpose, I will not slide again into despair. If I were to suppress myself and allow life's busyness to overcome me again, I could spin inside the familiar but utter discomfort of depression and anxiety I left. I expect it could be the same with you.

Repetition keeps us on track when we want to instill new habits. During the times when we're not sure we can rally the energy, we try anyway, because it feels good in the end.

Your meaning, passion, and purpose await their day in the glorious light of your fulfillment. Prepare to shine in brilliance.

22 LOVE'S LIGHT

Everything carries love . . .

WHEN MY FOCUS changes from writing my message of hope back to the cuddle chair, Mom has left. Instead, Grandma Mary waits for me. Pink and white blossoms decorate her light summer dress. Although she's always been lean, I notice a gentle daintiness about her. Her porcelain face glows effervescent. I glimpse an azure world within her sparkling eyes.

"Grandma, what do you want to tell me today?"

"I already told you how much your grandpa Rob helped me by cooking, cleaning, and caring for our children. He was a wonderful husband, but how he handled our kids sometimes created a tug of war within me."

She explains how Grandpa wanted what was best for their kids. He wanted things done a certain way, so he jumped on them to get it right, issuing orders and nit-picking at mistakes. I cringe and wonder *Was he a perfectionist, too?*

Grandma suggested he leave his military conduct at the naval yard. It wasn't just what Grandpa said, though. When their kids misbehaved, she watched him shake the living daylights out of them, take a strap to their behinds, and even kick one of them across the room. (Whitworth 2010)

Grandma reminds me about the trouble Grandpa and Bob had getting along. As she talks about him, my thoughts wander from her situation to mine. I refocus on Grandma to hear her say, "I worried for such a long time that I didn't create enough harmony. Eventually, I turned my problems over to the Lord. If I hadn't, it would've driven me nuts."

"Yeah, I've also blamed myself for the times when we lacked family togetherness."

We move on from her family's discord to talk about cultural and religious norms insisting "the woman's place was in the home." I remark how Mom, Grandma, and I represent three generations of successful, yet reluctant, career women.

Grandma smiles. "I loved tailoring. It satisfied a zeal for creating. Alterations offered jigsaw puzzles to finding fit, and designing clothing expressed beauty. Customers so appreciated when the tuck there or the nip here enhanced on the outside what they hoped projected from inside. I got the most enjoyment from helping people feel good about themselves."

I say, "I believe it's important women rear their children. So, I wish I'd stayed home, but I'm secretly kinda glad I didn't. I suspect I might've been bored."

She laughs. "No, you wouldn't. You would've found ways to keep both yourself and your kids interested."

"Maybe you're right," I say. But I'm not convinced.

I recall the many years I attended night classes to finish my bachelor's degree while I worked full-time. Later, I used my spare time to build a business with Gillis. I can see how my work accomplishments fueled workaholism. I put in long hours and often took projects home. At that time, I didn't know busyness kept my depression at bay.

Still sounds like a hollow excuse.

I roll my eyes, clack my tongue against the roof of my

mouth, and shake my head. "I became busy and inaccessible, like Mom. Just another form of abandoning my kids."

To catch my tears before they start, I glance away, stare at the ceiling, and dab my outer lids with my index fingers.

She puts my hands in hers. "My dear, nobody judges us more harshly than ourselves. You can't change anything from the past. Although, you now realize you can change how you feel about it."

She explains how we all carry burdens, but when we trust and allow the Lord to share the load and consider ourselves through unconditional love, we receive hope and healing.

I exhale but find tears still want to flow. This time, I allow them to trickle down my cheeks.

"Explore how you view your choices about working and why you harbor self-reproach. Remember, forgiveness holds the key."

Grandma's hands get warmer and her body increases in brilliance. I notice light spreads from left to right onto the walls behind her and the chair. Radiance covers everything. She exudes the most beautiful sheen. Everything dazzles in luminous white with indescribable transparency and luster.

"Why do you appear this way?"

"It's love in its purest form. Love is light. Light is what we see. Light within everything carries love, its messenger. The absence of light imparts darkness—fear."

As I immerse in the growing brilliance, I revisit the idea of light and fear as two polarities. When unbalanced, the other dominates. That must be why I use the three globes to visualize love, fear, and a blend to balance the two.

23 CHALLENGING CHOICES

I'm the one who needs to commit . . .

GRANDMA HAD ENCOURAGED me to reexamine my past decisions, but I didn't regard converting to full-time job status as a choice. I've postponed answering her question for weeks.

Finally, I reflect on defining events from my early twenties.

"Your husband will never work again." The doctor's diagnosis after an auto accident plunges me to the rescue. Convinced I must work for the rest of my life, I discard my childhood vow not to be a working mother.

I've been vilifying the accident for decades, but I admit it. I made a choice.

୦୫୨୦

My expectation around family includes a healthy marriage. Mom and Dad celebrated fifty-six years together. I wish for the same honor.

Similar to many other couples, Gillis and I bounced through cycles. Whenever simmering sentiments boiled over, I worried it may be the end. Neither of us used the word divorce, but it was my interpretation when we argued in the drama triangle. Divorce was what I most feared about our relationship.

During the decades before my recovery from depression just a few years ago, having a happy, harmonious family was the foundation of my life's meaning. I had not yet discovered a burning passion within. So, each time separation thoughts threatened, I tried in desperation to repair the unfixable.

This happened with almost clockwork precision in semi-annual cycles. Some years we skipped a sequence, but each time was as agonizing as the last. Accusations about what was wrong in the family flew from both sides but stuck to my shoulders. My mind rejected the idea I was at fault. I outwardly defended my position as blameless, but thoughts plagued me—perhaps everything *was* my responsibility. I was such a good problem solver otherwise. Yet, I couldn't resolve the issues in my family in the manner I yearned for.

We argued about our children, disciplinary differences, and how much pressure to apply or encouragement to offer regarding their life choices. He wanted my consistent support, so we would form a united front, but personality differences and cultural clashes as basic as insisting the kids greet us with "good morning," "good afternoon," and "good evening" instead of "hi," played their hands in our conflicts.

I instigated venomous volleys or braced for his. Long after each explosion, we each plucked pieces of emotional shrapnel. Secretly, I simmered with fanciful countermeasures I would never act on.

However, I could not clear the air as I should have. I am my mother's daughter. Passive-aggressive behavior hissed from my emotional pressure pot until reaching another boiling point months later. The battles resumed.

After twenty-six years of matrimony, we concluded: time

to relocate to his homeland, Nigeria. I displayed outward excitement but harbored covert resistance. I wondered what would happen if our familiar arguments took place in unfamiliar territory. I didn't want to leave everything and everyone I knew, move thousands of miles overseas, and risk us splitting up.

I wanted to force Gillis to commit and eradicate my doubts. He went ahead to prepare a place for us while I searched for a way to secure my peace of mind.

Months passed until one day, while in a state of quiet and deep reflection, my quest ended. In a burst of pure clarity, assurance began as a whisper until words formed a resounding message: *I can't force him to commit. I'm the one who needs to commit. I need to love unconditionally.* I realized the answer to the commitment I sought was not in Gillis's hands. It was in mine. Instead of focusing on barriers, I concentrated on how to mitigate risks. I began owning my insecurities about our future instead of projecting them onto him.

Soon afterward, I uprooted from family and friends, packed our possessions, and settled with him in Nigeria. Our crisis cycles slowed but did not stop. Old drama triangle patterns persisted.

Awareness created a first step in quieting my qualms, but I soon lost my sure footing, forgot to apply what I had learned, and floundered a few more years. I needed much more practice.

I wondered then why I seemed to love my children unconditionally but couldn't extend the same unbounded love to myself and my husband. Now, re-examining the past as Grandma prompted, I realize Gillis acts as my mirror. Our battlegrounds weren't really about him or our kids. I was fighting my own issues.

I couldn't offer him full, unconditional love until I marshaled it for myself.

24 ANCESTRAL APPRECIATION

A sense of linkage . . .

BACK IN MY childhood parlor, Grandma and Frances wait for me on the cuddle chair while Mom stands near them, by the window. I walk over to express thanks for their participation and inspiration in what I've been writing, but Grandma interrupts.

She reminds me of our talks and the common threads in our histories, scoots forward, and squeezes my hand. "You're learning the biggest lesson of all—forgiveness. I commend you for that. Viewing yourself through compassion and love keeps you on the right track. You've done much to be proud of so far."

"Thanks, Grandma."

I consider how much I've realized recently. When I focus on the issues, grief and anxiety engulf me. But as I let myself off the hook and learn to accept what is, or was, it changes how I feel. I'm getting better at letting go of problems and, instead, focusing on solutions. I still need regular practice, though. I appreciate her words of praise and encouragement. "I love you," I add.

Aunt Frances gets up and paces the floor. "That man lived in our village till he died. He acted as if nothing happened. After a while, I pretended the same. I shoved it aside like a bad dream.

"After I grew, I wanted to confront him, but his old threats stopped me. Who'd believe us against such a powerful bloke? I wondered if he harmed any other girls. I'd cringe and shudder at such ideas. I shoulda outed him, sure.

"I put the blame on me. Why was I stupid enough to stay? Why didn't I leave when Annie did?

"Some years later, Annie and I dredged up that day. When I told her the particulars, we both wept. Sorry for abandoning me, says she. But I never blamed her.

"A poison all my days. I tried to push it away, but it'd come back from time to time. Still, I married and bore childern. Probably mollycoddled them."

She washes her hands with invisible water and stands sideways by the mirror.

Aunt Frances and I discuss how we didn't trust ourselves and how irrational it sounds. That one time we didn't take action to prevent what happened made us believe we were destined for other poor decisions.

Although neither malefactor physically wounded us, emotional trauma ravaged us. We each believed we failed to protect ourselves from them. So, the outrage stayed with us, not only against them but also against ourselves.

We conclude that confronting Phil Joren allowed me to take action differently and fix the boundary he trampled that day, helping me to forgive both myself and him.

"You freed yourself."

I'm nodding my head as I say, "I appreciate your perspectives and insights. It all makes sense to me."

I walk toward Aunt Frances and take her hands. "I'm so pleased you told me your story. I'm enjoying getting to know you."

She smiles and gives me a squeeze before she lets go and settles on the piano bench.

I return to the cuddle chair, perch on its edge, and face Grandma. Gazing into her sky-blue eyes fills me with airy comfort. "To have this connection with you now makes me feel I didn't miss out."

Grandma beams, draws me into her arms, and holds me for what seems an eternity in mere minutes.

Smiling through my tears, I glance behind Grandma's shoulder to where Mom waits. I shift to look at them together: mother and daughter. What a special privilege to be with them this way.

Linkages among our histories and excitement about a growing sense of expression fills me.

25 INNER INSPIRATION

It cycles through my entire nucleus . . .

ALONE IN MY writing room several months later, I play a guided meditation. (Yensen 2014) A deep belly breath through my nose fills my diaphragm so full I can't contain any more air. I release as much as I can through my mouth. I exhale with an audible sigh to release worries of the day and relax my mind so I can summon inspiration.

After deep breathing, I plant my bare feet flat on the cool tile under my writing chair and imagine they grow roots as two trees. As trunks, my legs sprout roots and burrow, thirsting for a golden-white wellspring at the Earth's center.

Bright light pumps upward, inching near my feet. I welcome its luminous force into my soles and breathe again. My legs irradiate. My abdomen rises as it draws in air, rests to a count of three, and expels all resistance.

I draw breath large enough to fill an imaginary ruby balloon stretching and expanding beyond my rib cage and onto the floor. Light surges into my core, filling my heart with warmth. I rest a few seconds before it saturates my chest cavity. My heart pumps in a one-two-three-four rhythm while the golden-white essence circles and dances through my heart.

Again, a deep breath and release. Light travels to my throat, where I have found my voice. No longer suffocated, I have been speaking through my writing and poetry collections. Another deep breath pushes the illumination into my head. It bursts into a spray of fireworks above me, showering and landing around me. It cycles through my entire nucleus after it meets the ground, reabsorbs, and again travels through my earthy root system.

Am I weightless?

I lift my thoughts toward a baby-blue sky decorated with marshmallow silhouettes.

I remember as a child relaxing on the overgrown grass. The hand-powered mower stood propped against the whitewashed wall. Splotches of parched turf marked a reminder of unfinished watering chores but didn't distract my mind. I would stretch my arms and cross them behind my head, using them as a cushion. Cumulus shapes formed fluffy animals and other glorious forms seen only by me—my own Rorschach's wonder and amazement.

Once I spotted a shape and named it, the contours and curves drifted on as a new form.

Cloud watching passed the time in childhood summers. My playmates and I watched the same clouds but saw different things.

Isn't that like life?

Just as I can view my past differently, another person and I may perceive circumstances differently. The same event can appear sunny or shaded. It doesn't automatically make either right or wrong. When I describe my viewpoint to others, they may or may not recognize it. I may not spot theirs, either. Compassionate communication outside the polarizing drama triangle fosters a shared understanding.

When emotions run high, recognizing them becomes

crucial. I can either draw a clear boundary to talk later when it may be less upsetting or listen empathically. However, defending or insisting on my opinion during overwhelming reactions will not yield the results I want. People want to be heard. I need not agree with what they're saying. Recognizing which feelings are emerging can be as simple as a heartfelt restating of both the content and emotion behind the words. The other person can correct my summary if I'm mistaken. I consider it a shifting silhouette defined by the viewer. Neither the shape nor the perspective is incorrect.

The *communication* about the situation, event, or circumstance serves as the essential ingredient to this conversation. I allow the discussion to form with the whispered winds of empathy. Amid a calmer atmosphere, I can share my version.

This provides a way to navigate intense conversations full of powerful emotions. Although I, too, want to be heard, I can apply a method which doesn't depend on other peoples' abilities. Assuming the others aren't verbally abusive, I can allow them to continue speaking until they feel heard. It doesn't make me weak; it makes me strong because I develop patience and compassion. As I nurture my ability to see through others' eyes, it deepens a vision of myself. I create greater empathy and a healthier perspective about my situation.

Before long, my compassionate communication skills confront the ultimate test.

26 DRAMA'S DÉTENTE

The only deterrents I need...

THE SOUNDS OF water tumbling onto the shower tiles float into the bedroom and stir my senses. Still sleepy, I roll to my other side and cover my eyes with my arm. Last night's late hours on a consulting proposal justifies my wish for a few more winks. I drift between states of waking and snoozing. The combination of clothing rustling, heels clicking, and Aramis cologne wafting nudges my eyes open. Gillis stands dressed in a white Igbo-style suit and black fedora hat.

"I'll see you later." He strides away.

I wonder where he's zooming to this early on the weekend. I check the clock. Sleep deprivation eclipses my sense of time. Well after nine a.m., yet I'm not rested. But I can't sleep now. After the front door swings shut, I roll out of bed and dress.

Morning activities of preparing breakfast, writing, and editing fill the hours before Gillis returns. He marches to the bedroom, changes to a pair of shorts and a T-shirt, and beelines to the kitchen. No "good afternoon." No smile. No explanation. Will we return to our familiar battleground? Determined not to launch the first offense, I keep quiet and buttress mental reinforcements.

I decide to wait without using my conventional arsenal. I

hope to respond without tit-for-tat, playing neither on offense nor defense. I strap on an unseen armor of choosing responses and compassion as my shield and retreat to the bedroom.

Before long, he joins me and explains where he went and why. He lobs some verbal bombs across the burgundy bedspread. The casings may differ, but the content fueling their fire remains the same.

Again, he deems me too laissez-faire. He wants my unwavering support and a united front to persuade one of our adult kids to make an important life choice. He worries a wrong decision will result in devastating consequences for our child. Already, he grieves the loss of a picturesque future.

I hear the words and track their landings, as foundations tremble around me. However, the trenches don't swallow me today. I stand firm in this surreal moment as an observer. Emotional shrapnel misses its mark. The barrage continues unabated while I listen without interrupting.

Curious, I covertly examine unexploded bombshells. They're duds. They don't impact me as before. I remain aware genuine anguish forged them. I empathize with his distress, confirm his viewpoint without conceding, and wrap my responses in love. He feels heard.

After I ask Gillis if he's vented all his frustration and anger about the situation, he hurls an ultimatum.

In the past, I would think, *he means it this time.*

Today, I challenge that idea.

He's a man of action. If he meant it, would he want to talk for hours? Wouldn't he just leave?

I avoided the drama triangle with him, but my propagandizer starts. *He did leave one time . . .*

And I finally realize, I've been playing a trick on myself all this while. I've been focusing on the one time he left, not the more than thirty years we've been together.

I'm not going to play that stupid game with myself or with him. Not today. Not anymore.

I lean in. "Sorry, you're so upset. I want to help you, but not by agreeing. I can help you feel differently about it, though."

My peace offering catches his attention. I remind him how I conquered my depression by viewing matters differently and examining why they caused distress. I also assert acceptable emotional boundaries.

Conflict ceases. We reaffirm our desire to stay together and resolve our issues. Détente begins.

෴

I consider how I sat secure and protected with no actual onslaught to defend against. In the past, these external battles mirrored the defenses of what warred within me. Now, I command greater peace with myself; I need no shield from him. Choosing my response and offering love over fear are the only deterrents I need at my disposal.

This could have been another agonizing conversation; instead, I'm elated about my immersion into the compassion triangle and liberation from the drama triangle. I realize the transformational power over our tussles has been inside us all along. We can each choose how to respond.

I used to believe circumstances and other people created my problems. Therefore, I concluded I should seek solutions from others. So, I would search for ways to manipulate the outcome to fit the ideal in my head. The results were temporary and faded, leaving me empty. Others saw me as a perfectionist control freak.

The more I focused on others' behavior rather than mine, I had a harder time accepting what was happening. When the blues dragged me down, I also believed myself powerless. Weakness made me want to reclaim power, but I avoided working on my issues. Instead, I obsessed more and more about fixing other people and their problems (mostly family and close friends), as if rescuing them would save me, too. The harder I worked to change a person or situation, the more frustrated and powerless I became. I could never solve my turmoil trying to fix someone else's. The way to reduce my distress hinges on addressing root causes within.

Let me restate another way. I need to focus on what I *can* change—what's within my control, not what I *can't* change. I can take steps such as proposing we discuss later, listening with compassion, taking safety measures when traveling, exercising, and eating healthy. But I can *always* change how I *feel about* a person or situation, even when I'm unable to change the situation itself or the person's opinion or action.

At first, compassionate listening seemed almost impossible during the most painful conversations, but practicing when it was not as distressing strengthened me for heartrending times.

I vow: No more self-inflicted emotional wounds. No more pinning joy and happiness on imagined family harmony. Nirvana is not set in the future. Bliss is not an elusive goal post pushing farther away each time I approach. I create heaven on earth by accepting current circumstances and discovering ways to foster happiness now. I embrace the present.

Healing heartache starts with steps toward self-love. Others cannot hold hostage my worth and meaning.

Now, I derive value by taking care of myself and sharing with others in ways meaningful to me.

Nobody can speak with certainty about the future.

Whatever may happen, I choose a purpose-filled life. I will keep practicing responding within my control to express love and compassion both to myself and others.

27 OUTLOOK OPTING

We can always wield power . . .

MOM, GRANDMA, AND Aunt Frances relax on the cuddle chair. I scoot next to Mom and rest my head on her shoulder.

I calculate how old Mom would have been today. And I remember her birthday marks an anniversary for me, too. On what would have been her ninety-fifth birthday, I began writing the first manuscript of *From the Shadows*.

My mind juggles through jumbled words, frustrating my desire to express profound gratitude for Mom, Grandma, and Aunt Frances. So, I begin my ritual with Mom. I lift her hand and place it on my palm, tracing each elegant and slender finger from nail tip to knuckle. Age spots speckle otherwise creamy skin as I glide my fingertips back and forth. Each rub radiates more love and energy my way until I catch and hold calm and clarity.

I raise my head. "You've all deepened my understanding by sharing your stories to fuel forgiveness. Mom, I appreciate how your special day served to charm my first book out of me and became a catalyst for all our conversations now."

I look at Grandma. "You've been a remarkable contributor for *this* story, and I'm grateful for your guidance."

Grandma's soft gaze and tender smile travels directly to my heart and wraps me in a silky essence. I pause a moment to enjoy the sensation before focusing on Aunt Frances.

"I really appreciate how you—"

"I should be thanking you. When I was young, girls couldn't easily express ourselves. My story isn't for healing myself but for you and others. You're a voice for me now."

I squirm in my seat.

"I hope I do your story justice."

"Ah, sure you will. No worries there at all, at all."

Grandma changes the subject. "You know, a woman doesn't have to work to fear she's failed her children. Any mother can weigh herself down with guilt. We want women to learn how to free themselves from such a burden.

"All families struggle. Your mother thought of me as an angel, but I had very human flaws. Your uncle Bob figured I could've done more to influence my husband. I suspect a reason for their clashes stemmed from the similar sides of each other that neither one wanted to admit."

"Mm-hmm, Grandma, I get it. I call it the 'shadow' side."

We discuss the shadow sides of ourselves and how we want to deny them due to shame or guilt. When we become aware of and accept our imperfections, others' behavior bothers us less.

"So, you're saying Grandpa and Uncle Bob triggered these parts of each other, and it often created problems."

"Yes, my dear. Everyone has challenges in their life. How you deal with those ordeals can make you stronger and build trust in yourself. You can cope with whatever life throws your way."

Grandma takes my forearm, squeezes it, and flashes a big grin at me.

We talk about how I had rejected images and ideas that didn't conform to my false assumptions. For example, I thought taking professional risks was selfish. I presumed I should hold the "steady Eddie" role, like Mom, while Gillis pursued business ventures, like Dad. I beat up on myself over preferring my career to homemaking. I had been fooling myself by repeating flawed stories and selectively reinforcing my beliefs.

Now I have a more objective picture of my past, I understand what they're explaining better. Everyone experiences anguish. However, everything in life capable of inflicting pain also offers healing and growth. How I view the experiences will either hinder or help.

This idea poses another way of saying I can choose my response. All events offer decisions about how to act, no matter the situation, and can prove liberating. An example is my recent argument with Gillis.

Grandma says, "Well, you may doubt your power at times, yet the one thing we have absolute control over is our response."

That reminds me of an idea from Stephen Covey that when we can't change a situation, the only thing we can change is how we view it.

As we mull over the concept, it cements my biggest lesson in life: conscious response rather than unconscious reaction. Even when we see no option, with practice, we can always wield power over our mind and emotions.

I settle back into the chair's soft comfort and tap my toes together as I form my next thoughts.

Mom's lingering scent of hairspray mixed with her perfume conjures a musty sweetness. Her eyes gaze in pure love at mine.

I say, "I'm filled with such appreciation that you're with me on this journey. Thanks for inspiring me regularly to allow the words in our stories to pour through."

I continue to thank Mom for encouraging us as children to aspire to our dreams and setting an example for us by pursuing her passions. When she first began sketching as a child, she wasn't actually as good as she thought, but others didn't discourage her. So, she always encouraged us to try anything we wanted.

Until recently, I embraced everything through others' passions—vicariously. Mom excelled in singing, painting, editing, writing, and acting. I wondered what other creative pursuits were leftover for me, as if the supply were finite. Mom didn't make it a competition or a goal to measure up to her achievements. I did. I wanted to keep earning the love I already had. Worthiness no longer eludes me.

"I'm grateful we're collaborating and excited about what you're motivating me to share. Thanks, again." I nuzzle my nose and cheek against Mom.

"I love you," we both say. Our embrace tightens.

ॐ

For a long time, I wondered about events in life and how much to push against them.

When should we surrender to what happens?

What about diseases?

Should we fight or accept fate?

How do we choose which one?

I believe I have the answer to my long-standing questions and appreciate what it evokes in me. I should always search for joy and love in life because they're core to what I want. Whatever happens in opposition or contrast to my wishes can help me sharpen my focus on what I most desire. If an ailment afflicts me, I can refocus on being healthy and regaining wellness. Struggle against the current problem fuels a negative state of mind. Instead, by acknowledging the condition and concentrating on a solution, I can adjust my thoughts and emotions about it.

The idea you and I view life from our perspective, creating each experience unique to ourselves, has been around for some time. We don't see circumstances as *they* are. We understand things as *we* are. Works by G.T.W. Patrick, H.M. Tomlinson, Dr. Covey, and other writers include this maxim. We experience everything through our thoughts and feelings about it. We can view anything and anyone positively or negatively. A challenging situation provides an opportunity to sharpen the focus on what we truly want or expand our ability to learn and grow.

The best time to focus on my strongest desires happens when my vision of an idealized family seemingly disintegrates around me. As I concentrate on building and strengthening each of my relationships with Gillis, Victoria, Kenneth, and Christopher, my attention can shift to my behavior, my thoughts, and my emotions. I hold power only over myself.

How I perceive the world depends on how I interpret my experience. If I presume everything stays outside my control, I am a victim, a piece of wood bobbing around wherever the current and the waves toss me. However, if I realize I shape the situation through the way I perceive and respond to it, I handle a rudder. I use oars. I run an engine. I can steer where I wish. I flow on the current, but I navigate the direction, speed, and movement. I don't struggle upstream against the flux but instead glide downstream with the current. My thoughts and feelings about every situation become oars, rudders, and engines to steer and navigate.

I will respond outside a drama triangle by offering

compassion to myself first, then everyone else. To realize I can sustain joy forever regardless of circumstance, independent of what others do, and irrespective of my failures offers me liberation. Everything in life eases my learning and growing as I seek and create enjoyment and love.

FREEDOM THROUGH FORGIVENESS

Everyone can tap into a never-ending wellspring of deep and joyful connection

28 VICARIOUS VINDICATION

I dropped surrogate baggage . . .

INHALE UNTIL MY lungs cannot stuff any more air and blow out. I do this again two times from my writing chair. Now, I am in a state to receive whatever comes.

No cuddle chair today.

Instead, a setting comes to mind, inspired years ago during a guided visualization. (Howell 1999) I stand beneath shady trees. Lush grass lays a path before me. My bare soles crush nature's cool, green carpet beneath while individual blades spring straight between my toes.

Birds in high branches call to each other. Leafy chatter overhead intensifies in a flurry only trees can translate. Splotches of dazzling sunlight interrupt the pockets of shade shrouding limbs. Luxuriant branches and boughs from opposite sides of the trail form a calm canopy.

Along my right side, rough-hewn stones stacked together six or seven feet high beg me to trace their grooves with my fingertips. I presume artisans carved their centuries-old chunks to form the wall. Moss grows in the mortar between most of the rocks, suggesting frequent rains.

Mid-way along the wall stands a gate—an archway with a weathered deep brown, almost black, door matching its curve.

The iron handle on its right forms a lazy crescent. It resists my push, but a second attempt with my shoulder thrusts the door half-way open before it sticks in the ground.

A comforting lilac aroma and potpourri of other flowery fragrances shower me as I enter.

I glance past my immediate surroundings. About a football field length's away, the wall ends on my right and about the same distance on my left. Flowers span the bottom of each wall in bunches of yellow, purple, red, orange, white, and pink. I try to separate the daffodils from pansies, hibiscus, and other varieties before I realize they're too numerous to single out. Here and there, a few lush white and purple lilac bushes soar eight feet high. Assorted fruit trees also dot the landscape.

In the distance ahead, gentle rolls of turf, a round pavilion, and towering yellow, gray, and tan outcroppings block my view to gauge the sunny garden's full depth. I guesstimate the entire garden spans many acres. Eight roman columns form a glistening circle of marbled beige and cream, the sole support of the pavilion's dome cover. The front and back are open, but the sides are enclosed. Twin poplar trees stand at attention aside each of the front two columns.

Nearby and slightly to my left, a jacaranda tree stands heavy with sweet, purple blossoms. The grayish-brown trunk looks as wide as I am tall. Deep striations in the bark mark its maturity. Around its base, my favorite flowers, birds of paradise, flock in their beds and bathe in scattered sunshine. Sounds from the jacaranda's topmost branches draw my attention. Lanky white birds with s-curved necks and twittering orange beaks lodge there.

Toward my right, a wooden footbridge crosses a stream. The bridge's sleek bend and bright-red railings remind me of Chinese garden paintings. At the stream's source, a waterfall cascades over the rock formations, forming a cyan pool. The sparkling water invites me in. I undress and dip my toes to check its warmth before wading inside. I arch my spine and float. As I drift in relaxation, aches evaporate from my back.

I reflect on what I have been releasing and the process I have undergone. Over many months, I wrote in private, detailing the most distressing incidents with my children. And, I explored what about my conduct made me ashamed or long for forgiveness.

My aha moment struck me with a brilliant flash when I realized, I held myself responsible for things I didn't even do.

I rewrote each ordeal and isolated my part in the drama. I focused on *my* actions, *my* inactions, and *my* interactions.

But I wondered *why* I bore the brunt of so many issues within my family until I recalled how I had condemned myself about Phil.

Decades blaming myself for trusting Phil made way for many other episodes of judging myself accountable for others' actions. I excused others' behavior, made myself a martyr, and faulted myself.

I dealt with my mom guilt the same way I had handled passion—vicariously. I suffered as a surrogate.

I had believed I was not passionate about anything, so I adopted Gillis's, Victoria's, Kenneth's, and Christopher's dreams as mine. Similarly, I also adopted the blame for what I presumed were their issues with each other, real or not. But maybe I was only focusing on the ugly parts of their relationship and not the beautiful ones.

The compulsion to seek forgiveness about issues which didn't belong to me lifted as I dropped surrogate baggage.

After bringing my mind to the present scene, I unwind in the pool. I am not blameless, but I pledge to bear responsibility solely for my role. The splashes and gurgles pour calm inside my mind, inviting cleansing and refreshment.

After floating for a little while, I step under the waterfall. Its cascade massages my back with a gentle pulse. I untie knots from years of over-responsibility and release their emotional tethers. I'm altering how I view past events, separating what is mine versus what is not.

As I bounce-step through the water, my hair drips its own waterfall into the surface below. I ascend steps, grab a snowy-white towel to dry myself, and wring my hair. I don dry clothes and amble to the pavilion.

Cushions, pillows, and a round, paisley carpet wait for me in its middle. Light streams from a circular skylight, bathing me within its ring. I relax cross-legged and yearn for a complete reimmersion in my inner sun. One deep inhale, and the embers warm. A second breath fills my lungs and feeds a fervor in my chest. A third inhale fans fierce sapphire, diamond, ruby, and amber flames. Always twinkling in willingness, my power recharges. Inner and outer rays radiate and connect, bursting into a kaleidoscopic blaze.

My deepest desires reignite, refueled with the courage to resume my journey.

29 FINAL FORGIVENESS

I forgive myself for . . .

TAKE MY NEXT step by reading how Mom finally released her childhood anger and hurt harbored against her father, Grandpa Rob.

Mom's History/Diary: Excerpt Four

After he died, I decided I had to get over my negative feelings for my dad; I just couldn't carry that load of anger and resentment for the rest of my life, and he didn't deserve to have me feel that way. I had to take time to straighten myself out and ask his forgiveness.

I was busy. I had a job, and I still had two or three kids at home, but every time I was a little free, and I was alone, I would lie on the bed and think about my dad and the scares that I used to have because of the way he treated my brothers and because I was always afraid that he might do that to me. I had been so mad at him . . . because he made us feel scared! I guess we all felt the same way. Isn't that awful, for kids to carry those heavy burdens?

I remember at least three times over a period of about two or three years that I would stay on the bed and think about nothing else, and I finally got it out of my system. I got thinking of all the wonderful things that Dad had done for us, instead of all the things that I was angry about. And it lifted such a load off of me!

... He would go out of his way to see that we would have fun, even if he jumped all over us because we were doing it wrong! ... My dad and mother went up the canyon a lot for picnics and that sort of thing, and we always enjoyed ourselves ... He went out and threw big bucketsful of water all over the backyard, and when it froze, it made a good skating rink for us.

... I also remember being young enough to ride on his shoulders, and oh, boy, did I love those rides!

... When I think about my dad nowadays, I have learned to accept him for what he was and to think of what a wonderful father he was in so many, many, many, many ways. (Whitworth 2010)

I note Mom doesn't refer to Grandma Mary playing a role in this. It's between Mom and Grandpa Rob. The observation bolsters my recent insight into shedding proxied blame and emboldens me to explore further through practice.

With pen in hand, I draw deep breaths and scrawl about each shudder I need to set free.

I forgive myself for suffocating my writing passion for forty-eight years.

I forgive Beth for stuffing her desires and emotions into the shadowy cave.

I pause a few minutes to absorb the statements' full impact before continuing. The next one makes my body tremble.

I forgive Beth for her naiveté in trusting Phil's invitation to head upstairs.

Once I write these three affirmations, their intensity compels me to utter each word, accentuating the freedom. Calmness permeates the air a few moments.

My focus strays from the paper to my motherhood. As I recall several tempests, decades-old taunts start their scornful soundtrack.

The knot below my shoulder blade tightens, but I remain resolute and write out various statements, including:

> I forgive myself for not creating the nurturing home environment in the way I wanted it to exist.
>
> I forgive myself for working instead of protecting Kenneth when another child clobbered him with a brick at daycare.
>
> I forgive myself for neglecting to collect the kids from daycare that day.
>
> I forgive myself for leaving them alone as after-school, latch-key kids.
>
> I forgive myself for workaholic mania constantly delaying my evening arrivals.
>
> I forgive myself for creating an unhealthy home environment around my compulsive codependency and perfectionism.

As I revisit the most heart-wrenching incidents for each child, I plunge into excruciating detail about what I release. Lifeblood inks the fibers before I wash these kinds of stains. Finally:

> I forgive myself for working late and not going straight home on New Year's Eve when oil charred Christopher's arm and chest.

I forgive myself for leaving the door ajar when Kenneth crashed down the stairs.

I forgive myself for allowing Jerri to tend Victoria.

I forgive myself for *all* my failures as a mother.

It's time to step away from an elusive pedestal of perfection and form a different model around my question, *What kind of mother am I?*

I am a mother who had failures, but they do not make me a failure.

I am a mother whose children know she loves them even if they didn't always see it.

I am a mother who loves myself despite my imperfections. Yes, even my shadow side catalyzes learning and growing, keeping me keen to discover more. I am perfectly imperfect.

I am a mother who tried her best, and even with all my flaws, my children still love me.

I am a loving mother.

30 ELIZABETH'S ENOUGH

You are free . . .

RETURNING MY THOUGHTS inside the garden two or three days later, my eyes trace along the rough-hewn stones enclosing me within its grounds. I open the door, welcome Mom, and usher her into the surroundings.

We pass by purple and white lilac bushes. Their flowery fragrances float to my nostrils and remind me of lilacs at my childhood home. We cross the stream and head straight to the pavilion.

She and I sit cross-legged on a round, six-foot-wide paisley rug patterned with red, white, brown, black, and tan. I enjoy the day's silence interrupted only by the whispering leaves and birds' trilling. I have no idea what they're saying, and it doesn't matter. I'm here to amplify *my* inner voice. It's time for me to rest in the natural stillness of my mind.

I envision digging deep into my love for Mom, then draw on the unconditional love she offers me. As I relax, my core radiates brighter and brighter. My breaths fuel the energy into a massive effervescence around me. The passion I once denied now flames within me, energized by the rising unconditional self-love I achieve through forgiveness.

Brilliance from my heart center bursts from each pore

as sparkles. I notice the same energy emerges from Mom. Thousands of sparkles from her unconditional love for me and my expanding love for myself rise and glide around us as if they grew wings, crisscrossing paths and encircling me in healing.

Mom's voice sounds just as magical. "Do you know Frances means freedom? The Latin interpretation is *a free one*. Elizabeth *Frances*, you carry a freedom torch of self-expression, compassion, and love. You are free."

Bliss surges me to a new height of buoyant wonder and ease for an inestimable amount of time.

Still seated, I notice a small, brass bowl appears to my left, just outside the sparkles. I rest it on my left palm, dip my right index finger into its water, and watch the ripples. The bowl expands before it disappears, but I continue dipping my finger into the watery air. As I glide my finger, sensations of airborne waves cascade through the atmosphere. A melody invites a message. The pulsation floats beyond my hand and into my heart space. I marvel at the airy rhythms acting as ripples in water. Ecstasy throbs throughout my body before fading.

In the rug's center, a dazzling light draws my attention—the love ball. Mom now shimmers ethereal before me. She appears to float in luminous white, offers me the ball, and motions for me to place it in my chest. "You are enough. You have always been enough. You will always be enough."

I peer beyond the orb's surface and discern purple, teal, and yellow patterns and hues like a crystalline abalone. The design intensifies into paisley fractals. I examine the first layer and immerse deeper into its levels.

"The fractal represents your being enough," she says. "No matter how faintly or deeply you look, the pattern prompts you to remember you are enough, now and always."

Overcome with gratitude and joy, I thank her for again

bringing the love ball. She encourages me to focus on nurturing the radiant orb with loving thoughts whenever I want my inner light to expand and envelop me with the same bliss I enjoy now.

I explain how each day unfolds better and better. I've been focusing on what I appreciate before I sleep or when I wake up. I've been meditating and writing most days. These habits propel me. So much lifts from me. Even when immersed in logic and busyness, when I pause in the morning to prepare myself or end my day with appreciation, meditation, and writing, it helps so much.

Mom says, "Happy to hear it. You're ready now to discuss and absorb the rest."

We chat about her unconditional love helping me forgive parts of myself and how comforting it has been hearing Mom endured similar pangs of failure and guilt. We're not so different.

My experience with Phil shaped my conclusion Mom could have protected me if she had been at home, instead of at work. Now, I fully accept it was never possible. However, the idea she should have shielded me, and I should, therefore, protect my kids from all dangers grew into a fixation over my maternal failures. Christopher's oil burns, Kenneth's tumble down the stairs, Victoria's babysitter, and all the other incidents were burdens I carried by singlehandedly setting unrealistic expectations.

Mom advises me to revisit those kinds of scenes whenever necessary and foster my new habits.

My mind starts spinning in a different direction, and I voice fresh concerns. After all, self-development practices could bring to light new zingers I've hidden from myself. Not only that, I could play a part in others' pain I may not realize.

Because I would lack awareness of my offense, I would bear no conscious regret.

Before I get too entrenched in a bunch of negative "what ifs," Mom shushes me and suggests I express regret and convey compassion anytime someone alerts me I've hurt them. Most of all, I shouldn't immediately justify my actions.

She reminds me to seek understanding, Dr. Covey's fifth habit, in those situations. In the middle of an emotional outburst about how I caused pain, the other person won't want to hear my explanation. Initially, I should accept the person's genuine anguish, offer empathy, and allow expression. Then, if the individual is willing, and it seems appropriate, I can explain my point of view. Whether others forgive remains their decision. But offering to make amends and forgiving myself stays my responsibility.

Through everything Mom and I have discussed, I clearly see forgiveness starts with self. By forgiving myself and others, I change, not the experience. True healing stems from forgiving others, regardless of whether they ask or not. I may judge them undeserving, but that doesn't matter. If I don't, a perpetual victimized poison festers and pumps through me. I can still hold others accountable, but focusing on the pain keeps me from joy and bliss.

Resentment and anger also create a blocking mechanism, obscuring the love meant to flow through me and each one of us. Shame and guilt block bliss, too. When I dwell on the negatives, I spiral downward. That doesn't mean I should focus only on the positives. Admitting what's undesirable without wallowing or suppressing is the goal. I consider it the ability to weather whatever storm presents itself and say to myself, *I feel it. I acknowledge it, and I prevail because I endured it before. I've felt this way in the past and will return to my bliss. I accept I'm not where I want to be but will focus on what I want.* This creates more inspiration. This cultivates a fertile environment for reconciliation.

I conclude, "Talking through these concepts has helped solidify them in my mind. Thanks."

"There's more," she says. "Follow me."

As we pass through the garden's gate, we step directly into the foyer of my childhood home. I glance backward to check my bearings through the open front door. I still see inside the garden until Mom shuts the door, and my childhood front yard becomes the backdrop. We enter the parlor. Seated on the cuddle chair, Beth waits for us. Mom draws Beth from the seat and helps her onto the piano bench. With Mom in the middle, me to her left, and Beth to her right, we each gaze into the mirror spanning the wall above the piano.

Mom expresses admiration for my strength and courage in facing my worst fears and recalling the most painful events. "Look in this mirror at every stage of your life, about anything hurting you. At those times, say to yourself, 'I love me. I accept everything that's happened. My experiences shape who I am.'"

After I repeat her words, Mom resumes. "Now, take a big breath and concentrate on what I have to say next."

I draw in three deep breaths and allow the tingles to travel from my lungs through my belly, down my thighs and just below my knees. I gaze into her sparkling eyes. She caresses my hand.

"Most importantly, love yourself. You must love yourself beyond any other. You believe I love you more than anyone, but after all your efforts to heal, I'm merely a reflection of your self-love. Beth also represents self-love."

She describes the inspiration coming to me and how I attribute this to her, Grandma, and Aunt Frances, but I should know we connect to something much bigger: the source of infinite intelligence and love. Some call this the Lord while others call this the Divine or the Universe. She assures me everyone can tap into a never-ending wellspring of deep and joyful connection.

"I am your mother, and I am part of the Divine. But mostly I am Mom because this is who you need now."

She explains that when I ask my readers to imagine their most beloved, the image represents themselves in their most loving state. Everyone holds the capacity for immense self-love. Love overcomes loathing. To accept this ability within ourselves allows our light to shine. It requires practice, but anyone can do it just as I've done. This self-love gem, a sparkling treasure, can light everyone's path.

"Wait. So really you, Aunt Frances, and Grandma are all me, and I'm just talking to different parts of myself? Like my chats with Beth?"

"You could interpret it that way, but it's not an either-or thing. You're accessing the most loveable part of yourself through this whole experience. And we are inspiring you. And we are all aspects of the Divine."

Mom goes on to explain the cuddle chair's relaxed setting allowed my mind to freely explore possibilities. It's connected to the story I created about the puppy. Uninhibited imagination encouraged another perspective. My false belief I had nothing important to say and my cries for healing called Mom, Grandma, and Aunt Frances. I reconciled inner struggles by interweaving their histories with my past.

"You presumed you could not accomplish this alone, so we joined you. We shared our stories for your healing. You drew on three generations of women for strength and encouragement. You tapped into love's source. Others can tap into it, too. They can draw inspiration from their loved ones until they realize, as you do now, self-love can propel them and shine their way.

"At some point, they'll recognize love never abandons them. As they practice what they nurture, Divine love will always be there."

I draw in three more breaths and allow Beth and Mom to fade. My thoughts spin about what Mom's revealed. *Damn.* Already, I didn't want to admit to anyone how my dead relatives encourage me. *But how can they be both separate and a part of me? Seems downright looney.*

Let me try to focus on the inspiration and make sense of the parts I can. Our conversations took me through a maze of fear and self-love, exploring various aspects of myself. Mom, Grandma, and Aunt Frances helped me view myself and my burdens from new angles.

For example, Aunt Frances's ordeal enabled me to witness Phil's assault without judging myself. I don't condemn Aunt Frances for staying behind when Annie left. I don't fault Beth now, either.

I regard both Mom and Grandma doing what was necessary to help their husbands support their families. Working-mother blame and guilt acted as a symptom. Resentment against Mom working connected to Phil's assault. I recognize Mom never abandoned me. I also realize no matter how much I obsessed about protecting my children, my efforts would never erase what Phil did to me.

Mrs. Joren adopted blame for Phil. But she wasn't accountable for his wrongdoing.

Grandma and I carried vicarious guilt about our family dynamics thinking we were responsible for fixing them. But we are responsible solely for our own actions.

Mom put self-imposed limits around creative expression,

pigeonholing them as hobbies. She lived less constrained than Grandma and fulfilled Grandma's untried theatrical talents, that's for sure. But I've sidelined creative pursuits, like Mom. I can expand my writing beyond a hobby and treat it as a business. Time to truly embrace entrepreneurship.

Separate threads from my ancestors pass through me weaving a way to explain my narrative. Out of their histories, I reconcile with my past. To view other perspectives enables me to forgive myself and unravel the failures that threatened to strangle me all these decades.

However this whole thing has been happening I may not be fully able to explain, but I can't deny the incredible results. I manage to whisper a thank you.

Within my bosom, both my heart and the love orb glow. I can always keep these gifts with me. I am irreversibly happy. I am already enough. These are both entwined now.

No matter what, I can overcome any situation. When I fear I'm faltering or not progressing as I should, I'll follow the basic pattern. Breakthroughs happen when I step forward with happy habits and self-care. My self-love also expands. I truly trust myself.

I stretch out my arms, throw back my head, and revel in such a loving reflection. A new melodic refrain, *inspiration from my Frances forebears blend and mend in me,* hums in my head. Sunshine spins in my chest and twirls through my throat until its radiant beams dance on my curved lips.

Indeed, I am a free one.

31 CLEANSING COMPASSION

A healing session . . .

AFTER MY LIBERATION, a few months pass. As part of my self-care routine, I wonder about what else to reexamine from my past.

I'm prompted to visit Danny.

We relax on his patio chairs, enjoying the warm, afternoon air against our skin. Danny disassembles his rifles from today's target practice and lays the pieces on the table for oiling and cleaning.

We catch up with chit chat before I disclose why I'm eight thousand miles from home. I read introductory *From the Shadows* passages for context and skip to the part about Phil. I recount the incident precisely as I wrote it.

I notice his gun cleaning distraction stems the welling in his eyes we both pretend not to notice. I wonder if hearing about Phil pricks his conscience about what happened between us as thirteen-year-olds.

I thought I fully forgave Danny long ago, but I believe unconscious remnants were the reason I transformed into a Chimera those years before.

Danny branded it "fooling around," but I wouldn't describe it that way. I blamed myself for freezing instead of fleeing or fighting, although I suppose my tears and pleas stopped him.

Some part of me also clung to a victim identity—what I now realize was an unconscious connection to my earlier episode with Phil.

We never discussed in detail the day Danny and I were alone in the 5,000-square-foot house, and he pinned me down on the golden, crushed-velvet bedspread. Over forty years ago, Danny asked for and received my forgiveness. We both wrongly assumed we had completely shed that past and moved on.

Anticipating our conversation makes my heart pound in my throat and fills my body with elated tingles all at the same time. I wish for closure, not just for myself, but also for Danny.

His gun cleaning complete, the dusk's cooler air nudges us inside. We each settle into one of his brown leather couches. We're in his sanctuary surrounded by manly memorabilia. Twin televisions hang on the wall. I curl my legs under me and to one side while my body leans on a comfy cushion.

I don't need to read Danny the chapter about us. He was there. We continue our focus, instead, on Phil and speculate whether he was a serial pedophile. We worry about our childhood friends.

Danny cocks his head. "I wonder if Phil did anything to me? I don't remember anything. Maybe I've repressed it like you did, though."

We reminisce about our old neighborhood and childish antics. I reflect on sweet Johnny and how I'm unlocking unconditional love. Danny confesses he and a friend hid Johnny's bike.

We resume our discussion about the Joren family. Danny

maintains he's never ventured inside their house. A bit later, he describes their staircase.

I reveal something else to Danny. What happened between us as teenagers prompted changing my nickname from Beth to Liz. Almost overnight, the "fooling around" incident shifted my personality from carefree to controlled. Now, Danny grasps how that unconsciously triggered my earlier trauma caused by Phil.

Danny hangs his head and mutters how sorry he is.

I assure him I forgave him long ago, and I'm here to help us both heal.

Warm tears slide down my cheeks as I pause in silent empathy with him.

After my visit with Danny ends, I sit alone on the plane and gaze at the clouds. I remember the cat statues and surmise reshaping our past means I no longer need to consider the statues my guardians. My safe space doesn't rely on any thing or any place. I can create a sense of protection for myself.

I smile when I call to mind all the details of our conversation. My heart pulsates through every vein in appreciation. A healing session coming from love, not a judgmental paradigm, liberates us both.

Sharing my stories cements a profound and soulful purpose.

32 WHOLESOME HOMECOMING

It was always here . . .

As I conclude a visualization several weeks later, I leave the garden and close its arched door. No gateway to elsewhere today. Outside, I take in the scene when I sense Mom, Grandma, and Aunt Frances's unseen presence. I recognize them as part of the Divine. Part of me.

My freestyle musing activates. I walk to my right, past the garden's stone fence, until hillside stretches across all I see.

I survey the sweeping vista and notice wildflowers at every spot. They wave to me from bobbing florets swaying in the gentle wind. Yellow, orange, white, purple, pink, red, and blue—all scattered in a mottled rainbow. Soft and fragile, the flowers offer strength and medicinal power. Each represents something to me. For example, the daisy symbolizes innocence and purity. The wind carries their fragrance and tickles my nose with its sweet perfume. I inhale and drink it into my lungs.

Tender love vibrates as my heart beats in time to it. No sounds, not even soothing whispers, interrupt my relaxation and peace. Personal solitude.

During this leg of my journey, I recognize that wherever I

go, I can carry love with me. I may detect it more sometimes and less at others, but it always waits. Whenever I'm ready, I breathe and calm myself to hear these women's whispers and note the new path they've paved for me to follow in my way and time.

Gratitude springs from an eternal well of welcome. I will always appreciate them.

To the light within, I surrender.

Where I stand, luminosity travels through the planet's crust and mantle from a golden core. Rooted tendrils pump alongside earthy arteries and veins, sourcing light within all their capillaries until they join inside my feet. The healing glow travels upward through my legs. It rests momentarily in my pelvis and surrounds my belly button before pumping as lifeblood. I allow the sensation to breathe a few minutes as my heart softens and pulsates with the healing power of the white and golden light spinning inside the right side of my chest.

The upper half of my body emits an outer radiance. Its gleam travels through my throat and creates a heaviness in my forehead between my brows. I shut my eyes to revel in lidded visions of sparkling amethyst, amber, and quartz luminaries. The light passes onward to my crown. I open my eyes just before it explodes into a nova. Starry fragments shoot and stream through and around my body, encircling me.

My spirit recharges and rests as it enjoys another site of healing, inspiration, and intuitive guidance.

Three-year-old Beth emerges and darts toward me. She tugs on my hands to make me sit before she plops beside me. Her supple skin gleams with fresh sweat from playtime. Oversized, hand-me-down jeans dwarf her legs, but they're perfect for romping and army crawls with Danny and other playmates.

Her heart still beats fast, although her breath slows as she slides closer. We don't say anything for a few minutes as we savor each other's company.

My effervescence expands and encompasses Beth. I tuck one of Beth's stray tendrils behind her ear and beam at her, just as Mom usually does to me. How sweet and pure Beth seems.

"What do you wanna chat about today?" I say.

As the light encircles us, she shares words and wisdom beyond her years, drawing from infinite intelligence and eternal love.

"Be kind to yourself," she says. "You got so much to learn and do. It's not gonna happen all at once. You'll learn and grow forever. Life's got so many sides to it. Always look for 'em. No matter how good you feel, you can always feel better and better.

"Now, you're supposed to help other people with their problems. Just like you felt sad and didn't love yourself but got better, you're gonna help them, too. Guess I should say we. You see me sittin' here next to you, but I'm always a part of you. And we're both part of the Divine.

"You never lost your innocence. It was always here with me, waiting for you."

33 SHARED SPHERE

I am . . .

AFTER BETH'S ASSURANCE, I wipe tears from my cheeks and momentarily return attention to my writing room. Eyes still closed, my mind invokes gentle swaying and rhythmic clicking in tune to the latest music track pulsing from my laptop. My thoughts reroute.

I'm transported as a passenger within a train. Purple and teal blur by as it speeds forward. I glance out the window as images fade from my life's landscape. My journey has traveled so far and left much behind. The past dissipates in a flurry of light and dark. Scenes flash and fade so fast, almost subliminal messages to my mind. I'm engrossed in mental scenes and don't notice dim balls of fluorescent light perforating the darkness as the train moves through a tunnel to an underground station.

Screeching jolts my awareness back to my compartment. I rise and step to the ground after the train completes a full stop. Only stale air meets me. Chunks of gray rocks litter each side of the tracks and make me wobble. Dingy blue tiles cover the station walls until just before the ceiling curves, forty feet above. The station reverberates with echoes from the click, click, click of each passenger rushing across the platform to my right. I pay no attention to them.

I listen to the coach leaving on my left. Its electric hastening clack, clack, clack shifts to a fading hum before it blends into the night's stillness. I notice a hazy, yellow beam coming toward me but stand immobile aside the tracks. The syncopated and steady beat of another engine hums louder as it nears.

I hesitate at this routine line. I recognize where it leads.

On a train, I was a passenger observing fuzzy images of night and day along its sides. I kept my gaze to the right or left and watched what was ahead transform into the present then the past.

The oncoming train menaces closer, now. It whistles me out of its way. I rouse my legs from their snooze in this position. One step and another until all my limbs lighten with wakefulness. The train sprints its approach. Freedom surges me up the steps away from the track. I stand square-shouldered with my feet planted near the platform's edge as I watch the Pullman breeze past.

To those passengers, I represent a fleeting moment. The future changes to present as their blurry faces vanish. I've been where they're going and returned. I need not pass there again and again. Although I've summoned inner strength onto this platform, I linger until I gather the confidence to leave the station this time.

The gray metal railing in the middle of the stairs meets my hands with a cold clasp. I steady and propel my upward ascent. Almost gliding, I scale the steps two at a time. My nostrils flare, detecting a sweet odor in the air. The scent of new-fallen rain; I drink its moisture in a deep gulp.

I emerge into the midday sunlight. My pupils retreat at the rays' bright burn. I glance around for city landmarks, but they are no more.

I embark on the final phase of a journey without end. My future follows no laid track. I lay them with my bare feet in the blue-green grass of my thoughts and imagination. Behind me, the station folds into itself, collapsing in time and space.

All around me, nature's green grandeur flourishes with picture-perfect clouds bordering the azure sky. I'm not Dorothy, and no yellow brick road guides me. I pause, gulp the fresh air, and close my eyes for internal navigation. My soul prompts me to start left toward my new way.

My feet root like saplings, connect with the verdant land, and release. Again, I step. Roots penetrate the earth, creating more linkages.

These dappled sprouts do not slow me down. They grow with each step and trail behind, connecting me to the earth. I stroll grounded, centered, and natural. Shoots dangle from my soles and illuminate multihued tendrils.

Where my imprints were, flowers spring in their wake as brilliant shades of fuchsia, magenta, turquoise, and lemon. Low-lying ivory flowers sprinkle the meandering meadow along with orange fronds beckoning bees for a hearty pollen harvest.

As I stand on a slight incline, I notice a round cottage. Stones hewn from the nearby hills form its walls. Thatch covers zinc, producing double layers of protection from rain and sun. The tawny and cream stones invite me even before I smell pine smoke wafting from the chimney. Its smoke crosses the clearing until the forest's thick edge swallows it.

I finish sauntering through the field and arrive at the dwelling's large, curved-top door. The dark edge between the slats shows how much its medium-brown face faded over the years, but a sturdy wrought iron handle on the left grins with black lips. In the door's forehead, a cyclops knocker dangles, the same color and material as the handle. I lift and allow it to strike the metal plate below with a resounding clank. I strike the plate twice more for good measure. I enjoy things in threes.

I perceive soft shuffles moving toward the entrance. A woman's reedy voice from inside says, "Is it you?"

My eyes widen and right eyebrow raises. *Who is she expecting? Who exactly does she think "you" is?*

Myriad retorts zoom through my thoughts, but a single response shapes my lips and tumbles from my tongue. "I am."

Metal on metal grates and slides, concluding in a muffled clink before she swings open the door to its full width. Before me stands a woman less than five feet tall, almost a foot shorter than me. I suspect she has never been tall, but in her advanced age and hunched shoulders, she stoops even smaller. Thick, snowy-white hair sweeps back into an untidy knot. Loose strands hang on all sides. Lavender permeates the air with its welcome.

She invites me in and shows me to a russet couch. Paisley needlepoint encases its pillows, which indicates to me this must be the correct place. From the outside, the cottage appears centuries-old. However, the interior sports cinnamon-colored floorboards and modern, stainless-steel appliances. I try in vain to reconcile the contrast between the inside and outside, not just in décor but also in size.

The parlor area surpasses the entire exterior cottage capacity. Also, I notice several doors leading to other rooms and at least two hallways. I chalk it up to a visual trick on my eyes. It doesn't matter and isn't essential to my visit with the old woman.

She ambles to a stone fireplace and hearth situated behind us. Marbled rocks of muted blues, greens, grays, and tans glisten from old lacquer. The fire licks the logs with yellow, blue, and red flames in a comforting curl. About two feet from the blaze, she shifts a single flagstone from where it rests. She reaches into the opening. The hole swallows the entire length of her arms as she fumbles for a way to surface its contents. She grunts and her neck muscles strain as she lifts the object. It's a wooden box as big as her torso. She tugs the hemp handles on each side as she positions it on the floor.

I guess she's been caretaking the item, but I wait in silence for whatever protocol she deems necessary. I resist the urge to lend assistance, even though the box appears too heavy for her to carry. I sense I should stay put. She drags the container along the floor. Scratch marks gouge the floorboards, creating tracks toward us.

Out of breath from the exertion, she collapses beside me onto the couch with a muffled thud. I offer to get her water, but she shakes her head.

"It has never been this heavy."

She offers no further explanation.

I don't pry. I hope she'll provide more details whenever ready.

Uninhibited by my presence, she chants in a soft and steady voice. She breathes in deep through her nose, expands her diaphragm, and expels the air with a "huuu-waaa."

She repeats the inhale, exhale, and huuu-waaa in three sets of three. I breathe in threes, too, but in silence.

Something within the wooden box radiates through the slats like a bulb turned from dim to full strength.

In an elegant language I can't identify, she croons rapid-fire. She keeps her lids shut while her head nods now and then. Her head keeps bobbing, although she falls silent. I wonder if I should close my eyes, too, but I don't want to miss any part of what she might want to discuss with me. I stay on alert for at least ten minutes.

She expels the entire capacity of her lungs, mixing a sigh with a moan and swivels toward me. "Do you have any idea why this box glows?"

"Nope."

"This is light within. This is *your* light within. It's heavier than it has ever been. I've been preserving it for you, you know."

Why would she keep my light within? I already tucked that globe under my right breast. Mom gave it to me. Besides, why would it gain weight?

"This light within I've stored for you because I *am* you. So, in fact, you safeguarded it yourself the whole time. As you progressed with your self-development, it has grown in strength and waited for you to be ready. We all carry a light within, but this one is different. It's made for sharing. That's why it's so heavy."

My mouth drops open.

She barrels on and explains the sharing light within reignites souls who may seek me for their own illumination. They, in turn, share and spark blazes in others—perpetuating an infinite fractal.

"You carry a light within, and I pass you this sharing light within. You, therefore, say, 'I am,' and you hand the globe like a baton to the next person. It continues infinitely. Its source ignites from the heart or hearth."

She gestures toward the fireplace. "This flame is a special one, forged in desolation's ashes. I tended to the fire until it burned with a certain intensity, and you were ready."

Her eyes search my face for dawning comprehension before she resumes.

"Remove it from the box and place it near your heart. It will last forever."

She rests her hand on mine.

"I am, and you are. We are. You have always been and will always be. We are the same aspect of the Divine."

The Light Within

I half accept what she says, but I'm still absorbing the whole Mom, Grandma, and Aunt Frances thing. This is another level of freakiness. Yet, her words soothe my soul.

The woman explains she symbolizes a guardian self who nurtured this light throughout my darkest days. Accepting this sharing light within allows for the rebirth of not only myself but also everyone ready to receive inspirational messages, blaze their own trail, and spread it onward.

"Are you ready to embrace this light?"

"Yes."

I bend down to transfer the box to my side of the couch. When I yank the ropes, I brace to heft its load, but I'm taken aback and almost fall from inertia, so effortless is its mass.

The old woman chuckles. "Sorry, I should have warned you. I find the light awkward because it's not my place to carry it. The load is easy for whoever does the sharing. It will never burden you. It's only cumbersome to someone not meant to carry it."

I tilt my head and frown.

"It's true. You and I are the same. Yes, so you would assume I can, therefore, carry it as easily as you, but this orb is exclusive to you at this moment. Time and space bend and we can converse, but nothing is identical. Of all the limitless variations, this is a distinct instance and place, and thus a unique sphere."

While lifting it from the basket, I rub my hands around its smooth surface. It seems larger than the love ball and shimmers a brilliant white and yellowish glow. I wince from its brilliance. In my palms, it pulsates with a life force of its own.

She reads my thoughts—or so it seems. "It throbs with heartfelt healing and protection. This sharing light beats in excitement. The gentle tempo soothes and embraces. It is love.

Love and light are together. This is what you share. Whenever you illuminate and share, love heals, grows, shines, and spreads."

The corners of her wrinkled mouth curl.

Now, I understand. I'm to shine this light within for encouraging others to cultivate healing. I put the orb back in the box.

She grabs my arm. "No. No. No. It doesn't belong there anymore. It's for you to keep. Can you guess where it goes?"

At first, I want to say no but impulse kicks in. "Is it for me to place under my left breast?" I form it as a question, but as soon as the words tumble out, I realize it should be a statement.

I don't even wait for her to show she agrees before I again cuddle it in my palms. It warms to match my body's temperature. As I draw it to my chest, it morphs and absorbs. My skin appears almost translucent in my chest and my clothing transparent. My organs prepare space. I arrange it in a snug and secure spot.

From my bosom, the globe continues to glow through my skin and beyond. I glimmer throughout my body, although with brighter spots under both breasts. I turn to the woman to thank her, but I don't see her anymore.

My eyes search the room, scanning for her presence. Instead, I detect a faint lavender scent lingering a farewell. The room transforms in size, shape, and colors until I remember I've been relaxing on the guest bed in my writing room. For the past hour, I've been musing. My eyes still shut, my actual room and furnishings now reshape my surroundings.

I expand and contract my lungs in three successive deep, cleansing breaths. I wiggle my toes and fingers and open my eyes.

I am ready to share.

REFLECT AND RESPOND

You possess more resilience, drive, determination, heart, soul, strength, and love than you may realize. It all lies within you.

Let's ignite your inner light. Allow your wholeness to glow.

These pages pose questions and offer suggestions. Take time to reflect and write your responses to them. This is *your* journey.

As you progress through each section, be gentle on yourself. Don't rush through the questions in one sitting. Give yourself time. And don't try this process alone. Reach out to others. Besides discussions with your loved ones, consider using a professional counselor or coach when possible. I shared my insights and worries with an intimate network of family and friends as well as a coach. Schedule a discovery call with me to see if my coaching style suits you: www.habitualhappinesshub.com/hhhcalendar

As a complement to several of these practices, I've created guided visualizations and a printable practice guide. Access them from my website: www.ElizabethOnyeabor.com/gifts.

Walk with me now. Trust yourself in this process. As we travel together, you can heal.

PRACTICE 1: HEALING HER-STORY AND HIS-STORY

History's etymology is a "learned, wise man." The past provides insights. Wisdom emerges when we redefine what happened through a curiosity lens. After I revisited my incident with Phil and lambasted him, I created the puppy story. How we judge events can change not because we concoct a fairy-tale version but from allowing ourselves to explore a different viewpoint. This new perspective helps us look at it without as much pain.

This is a way of rewriting your her-story or his-story.

Don't get me wrong. I'm not advocating you suppress. I'm encouraging you to deal with the memories gradually and gently.

During my chronic depression, irrational thoughts screamed what a horrible, failed mother I was. However, my logical side knew how lopsided that story was. Part of my healing included writing about the agony I suppressed in a way I could handle it.

This is the reason for a trip to imagination land.

If you watched the movie *The Waterboy* (Sandler, et al. 1998), Bob Boucher (Adam Sandler) suggested a similar way for Coach Klein (Henry Winkler) to shift the anxiety and stress caused by his long-time bully and rival, Coach Red Beaulieu (Jerry Reed). Boucher recommended Klein imagine something soothing to replace Beaulieu's intimidating look. Klein pictured Beaulieu with a big baby's head. When Klein created this cute image for Beaulieu, he babbled giggles and coos with baby Beaulieu. Klein's stress left him, and his angst about Coach Beaulieu dissipated, allowing a breakthrough.

Neuroscientists at New York University published their research in Nature magazine concluding memories aren't static. What we remember strengthens through a method called "reconsolidation"—each time we recall an event, our brain rewrites it with added information. Reconsolidating troubling experiences shows we can influence our mind by encouraging the brain to include other, less painful associations. The new data allows the pain to release. (Schiller 2009)

Confronting what someone has done to you doesn't require you to face him or her in person. I recreated Phil in my visualization, yelled at him, and told him off—all part of my healing. I allowed myself to grieve losing my innocence and suffocating my passion.

I cannot change what happened.

I can change how I *feel* about what happened.

By asking, *How would I replay or replace the terrible scene with something less upsetting?*, I rewrote the traumatic story about Phil into the puppy story. I kept key elements but swapped out the most painful parts for something pleasant.

For each of the following steps, write on unlined sheets of paper (if possible) and record your thoughts as fast as you can. Ignore spelling and grammar errors.

Don't judge what you write or say while you're in the

process. Pay attention to your feelings and any physical sensations and describe them.

Time yourself. Spend fifteen to twenty minutes on each step. Gauge your comfort/discomfort level after each. If needed, recharge by doing something lighter you enjoy before continuing. Although you'll want to limit the time spent writing, as a whole, the seven steps have no time limit. This practice could take minutes, hours, days, or weeks before you move from one step to the next.

1. *Choose an upsetting incident where you felt wronged.*

   What persists as an upsetting incident where someone unjustly wronged you? Don't choose the most upsetting incident yet. Choose a scene that pops into your mind or bothers you from time to time. We'll call this person who wronged you the "offender."

2. *Picture yourself (and a companion) as protectors.*

   Imagine yourself as an older, wiser version, capable of protecting and comforting your younger self. We'll call this your "Sage Self." You may wish to select a beloved companion in addition to your sage self. We'll call this companion your "Beloved."

   Your Beloved could be a family member or friend (alive or dead), deity, angel, or a pet with a fairy-tale-like ability to understand you and speak.

   You and your sage self (and your beloved, if you choose this companion) will revisit the upsetting incident from step one as observers.

   Set your timer and write about the experience in as much detail as you can handle. Notice the discomfort as a reflection tool. Don't go so deep you get stuck but allow a little soreness as you strengthen emotional muscles.

Stop writing when the timer goes off, leave the scene, and thank your sage self (and your beloved) for the support.

3. *Rate your comfort vs. discomfort level.*

   On a scale of one to ten, rate your current level of distress about what happened (one would be slightly uncomfortable and ten would be completely uncomfortable).

4. *Confront the offender in a safe, imaginary setting.*

   With your sage self (and your beloved), create an *imaginary* setting where you can safely confront your offender (from the step one incident). You can substitute a chair or a pillow for the person.

   Set the timer and tell the offender how he or she hurt you. To say the words aloud is more powerful, but if lack of privacy presents a problem, you can also visualize the conversation in your head.

   Stop when the timer goes off, leave the scene, and thank your sage self (and your beloved) for the help.

   Consider writing down or drawing the scene afterward to capture what you experienced.

5. *Write an alternate reality.*

   With your sage self (and your beloved), set the timer, and revisit the scene from step one with as many upbeat replacements as possible. This acts to let go of the upsetting aspects through reconsolidation. This is similar to my puppy story with Phil.

6. *Write how steps one through five felt.*

   No need to bring your sage self or your beloved this time. Take this opportunity to process your experience of steps one through five, and explore any insights you may have gained. You may want to complete this statement and continue writing whatever comes to you: "I learned from this experience that . . ."

7. *Rate comfort vs. discomfort level.*

   On a scale of one to ten, rate your current level of distress about the original scene you selected in step one.

After days or weeks, try these seven steps again. Painful memories burrow deep and do not easily uproot. They grow back. Check your before and after ratings as a guide to decide whether to revisit these seven steps.

Discomfort may linger, but you will likely discover a shift in its intensity.

PRACTICE 2:
BEARING BURDENS

Like storm clouds heavy with moisture, emotional loads may weigh you down. When dark clouds unload their rain, they lighten and allow clear skies and sunshine. Similarly, you can release emotions and feel lighter.

Much of depression is suppression—not expressing upsetting feelings—and ruminating on them, instead. We can wallow in the past or obsess about the future, but it's different from airing the emotion.

You can express emotions through drawing, music, dance, writing, speaking, or any of the creative arts. You don't need to reveal to anyone else if you're not comfortable sharing yet. You can try these kinds of activities in the privacy of your home or room when nobody else can hear you. Write or draw your feelings on paper or a computer—wherever seems most convenient.

When I stress, the area under my right shoulder blade easily twists into a stabbing knot. I stretch, exercise, and self-massage with a tennis ball. I also explore the emotional sources of my tension.

Over-responsibility has burdened me. I learned to shoulder others' problems and carried those along with my guilt. Also, when Phil crushed my chest, his elbow acted as an impaler, pinning me down. That very spot on my back opposite my chest troubles me the most. By identifying Phil and over-responsibility as two root sources of pain, my flare-ups have significantly reduced and almost disappeared.

For the following steps, time yourself for fifteen or twenty minutes, and write your reactions.

1. *Breathe deeply.*

    Draw in deep, belly breaths and pay attention to the spots where you physically ache.

2. *Notice and name.*

    Name the painful locations in your body.

3. *Trace pain's roots.*

    Consider whether any physical discomfort links to your her-story or his-tory memory (Practice 1) or another incident.

4. *Link labels with aches.*

    What word associations jump to mind as you allow yourself to sense and describe your body's pain?

    When you acknowledge the sensations, you can begin releasing them.

PRACTICE 3:
AGED ASSURANCE

No amount of obsessing over the past changes what happened. You already know this intellectually, but accepting it emotionally can be tricky.

I blamed myself for trusting Phil and going to his room. I thought I should have done more, such as screaming at him. Instead, I fell silent.

Even though I didn't recall what happened for forty-eight years, that freeze reaction made me distrust my decisions as a teen and adult. Now, I've explored the scene from different angles and offered empathy to my six-year-old self. I've also allowed healing and regained self-trust.

How you revisit the past can shift how you view yourself in the present and future. Although the incident won't change, your self-judgments around it can.

Consider these questions and write out whatever surfaces. This is not about self-criticism but reflections from a heartfelt standpoint. When you look through a lens of compassion, you may find, as I did, that it was not possible to have acted differently. What if you believed you did the best you could under the circumstances?

1. *Identify an incident with lingering self-blame.*

   Do you place any lingering blame on yourself for what happened during the event you described in Practice 1 (Healing Her-story and His-story)? If not, perhaps another incident troubles you.

2. *Write your fault-finding.*

   Write your fault-finding linked to the incident in step one.

3. *Revisit the scene.*

   Revisit the scene with your sage self (and your beloved, if you wish). Hold your younger self's hand or provide comfort however you choose.

4. *Reassure yourself with compassion.*

   With your sage self (and your beloved), use a lens of compassion. Reassure your younger self in ways that help you lessen self-reproach.

PRACTICE 4:
FORGING THROUGH FIVE

Besides the incident from Practice 1 (Healing Her-story and His-story), what else troubles you, and who does it involve? Who could you forgive to rid yourself of the pain you carry because of them? Remember, it's not about whether the other person *deserves* forgiveness or not. Forgiveness is for you.

1. *Recall five hurtful situations.*

    Recollect past situations and the people involved that caused you pain. Write the first five events you recall. Briefly describe the circumstances and what happened. Do not go into any details that could retraumatize you.

2. *Rate your level of discomfort.*

    On a scale of one to ten, rate your level of discomfort with each incident.

3. *Process your emotions about one.*

    Choose one of the five incidents and use Practices 1 through 3 (Healing Her-story and His-story, Bearing Burdens, and Aged Assurance) to work through your emotions about it. We'll also use one of these incidents for Practice 6 (Deltoid Dialog).

PRACTICE 5:
CAGED CONDITIONING

Dreams we don't dare to envision can trap us in a prison of our own limitations. Psychologists call this learned helplessness.

You may have heard a story used in motivational talks about captive elephants who don't break free of mental shackles. Trainers tie a rope around a baby elephant's leg. The calf struggles but cannot break free. After a while, the baby elephant grows accustomed to the certainty of its bondage and stops trying. The trainer continues to restrain the mature elephant the same way. Although the powerful adult can untether the restraint, it makes no effort to do so. Similar experiments by psychologist Martin Seligman with dogs and shocks also demonstrated learned helplessness. (Seligman 1972)

When we suppose circumstances fall outside our control, we may imagine nothing we do could change the outcome. This conditioning continues after the situation changes and those barriers lift. We have stopped trying and remain confined to our inner limitations.

I didn't acknowledge writing as a serious interest until I was fifty-one. Over decades, I had dismissed the idea of being a writer as too far-fetched. For me to believe it was possible took time. However, the idea rooted and began to grow. I was excited when I wrote my first poem. I didn't think it was good enough, but I continued writing because it felt good. Another year passed, and I had created over fifty poems. By the third year, I had composed a draft of my first book, *From the Shadows*. It's a bestseller and includes that first poem.

Do you place a mental cage around certain things because you don't think they're good enough?

What if those constraints no longer existed? What could you do then?

1. *Give yourself permission to fly.*

    Ask yourself: No matter how outlandish it may sound, if I had a magic wand, I would . . .

    Fill in the blank.

    You don't need to figure out the *how* and *when*, yet. Just focus on the *what*.

PRACTICE 6:
DELTOID DIALOG

ANALYZE PAINFUL INTERACTIONS by revisiting dialog from the drama triangle. Dissect each role, see at what spot the drama started, when the roles changed, and why.

It's okay to see yourself as the persecutor. It's all right to view yourself as the rescuer. It's fine to see yourself as the victim. We regularly play *all* these roles.

When we play in the drama triangle and offend someone, the fastest way to step out of it is through an apology or expressing remorse. Conversely, if somebody upsets us, we can call the person's attention to the issue, either in the moment or at an appropriate time afterward.

Here's sample dialog from a minor argument. First, we show the original drama triangle dialog. Second, we reframe the same situation within the compassion triangle using an apology.

Drama Triangle Dialog

    Me: Why did you eat all the rice? (persecutor)

    Her: You should've told me you wanted it. (initially, the victim but in defense replies as persecutor)

    Me: I was saving it for later. (victim)

Her: Make some more. It won't take more than fifteen minutes. (rescuer)

Me: I don't feel like cooking anything. (victim) You're so inconsiderate! (persecutor)

Compassion Triangle Dialog

Me: Why did you eat all the rice? (persecutor)

Her: Oh, did you want it? (explicitly clarifying to avoid the drama triangle)

Me: Yeah, I was saving it for later. (victim wishing to return to the drama triangle)

Her: Sorry. I would have saved it for you if I'd known. (enters compassion triangle by expressing remorse)

1. *Select an incident from Practice 4 (Forging Through Five).*

   Pick one of the five incidents to explore interpersonal reactions during part of the episode.

2. *Write out a portion of the incident as dialog.*

   To the extent you can recall, script a portion of the conversation from an incident in Practice 4 (Forging Through Five), including quotes of specific dialog—whatever you remember about who said what. It doesn't need to be precise.

3. *Label the roles.*

   Identify who played the victim, the persecutor, and the rescuer during the sequence. These roles change as the drama intensifies. Sometimes the role says nothing until it moves to another position (e.g. from victim to persecutor or victim to rescuer).

4. *Which roles did you play?*

    Which role did you start in? Did you stay primarily in one role or did you often interchange among persecutor, rescuer, and victim? See where you acted most of the time. Identify where and when you flipped. Notice how the drama escalated, especially when the victim turned into the persecutor.

5. *Write your reaction to analyzing the dialog.*

    How did this analysis feel? Were there any insights or aha moments from writing the roles and dialog?

6. *Rewrite empowered, compassionate dialog.*

    Consider how the conversation could have evolved if you had responded from an empowered, compassionate standpoint, instead of playing in the drama triangle.

These are unconscious games we learned in our youth. We watched adults play these games and quickly picked up on the unwritten rules. It has continued generations upon generations. However, you hold the power to begin a shift that acts as an example for others and enhances interpersonal dynamics.

Study the recurring patterns. You don't play persecutor, victim, and rescuer just with yourself and loved ones. You also play at work on interpersonal and organizational levels. It even happens between companies and nations.

Start with awareness. As you practice, you can develop greater skill and will find it easier and easier to step out of the drama and eventually avoid it more and more.

PRACTICE 7: COMFORTING CARESS

IMAGINE YOURSELF AGAIN with your beloved companion near you.

1. *Describe your beloved.*

   Close your eyes to picture him or her in your mind's eye. Describe every aspect. What color is the hair or fur? What about the eyes? Maybe you hold hands or paws or give each other a hug or nuzzle. When you touch, what sensations come to mind? Do you attribute a natural essence to him or her? What fragrance infuses your senses? What loving or playful nickname does he or she call you? When your beloved says your name, what is the voice's timbre? Wrap these sensations around you in a comforting caress.

2. *Ask your beloved questions.*

   Once you envision your beloved, ask this question: What is it you love most about me?

   After you ask each question, allow your beloved to speak uninterrupted.

3. *Reveal a secret to your beloved.*

   Tell your beloved something embarrassing. Possibly, it's related to an incident in Practice 4 (Forging Through

Five). In response, imagine your beloved says, "I love you, unconditionally."

4. *Allow caressing, acceptance, and adoration from your beloved.*

    Envision your beloved gently caressing you in a manner unique between you. Perhaps your beloved holds your hand and strokes the back of it with his or her thumb. Maybe he or she tucks a tendril of your hair behind an ear, brushes bangs from your forehead, or traces a fingertip along your cheek and down your jawline. Create an affectionate moment between you. Let his or her adoration and acceptance rest with you a few moments.

5. *Follow-up question (optional).*

    If you find your mind wants to discount what your beloved says, ask him or her: Even though you know my secret, how can you still love me? Afterward, allow your beloved to immerse you in the most loving of assurances.

6. *Thank and note.*

    When completed, thank your beloved for the love and support, and allow his or her image to fade. Note any essential details from your conversation.

    Deep inside, you're nourishing self-love.

PRACTICE 8: SOOTHING SELF-COMPASSION

IF AT ANY point, your inner critic screams or swears at you, instruct it to quiet down. It'll get its chance to talk in Practice 9 (Propagandizing Prattle). We don't want to ignore the critical chatter forever, but we want to establish beneficial boundaries first.

Now, return to the conversation from Practice 7 (Comforting Caress).

1. *Relax.*

    When you're ready, draw in a deep breath. Allow your belly to expand. Let go with an audible exhale to release any negativity. Repeat two times or more.

2. *Reflect.*

    Recall the time you spent with your beloved in the last practice. Reflect on what he or she said and the influence on you.

3. *Turn banter into bubbles.*

    Anytime worrisome words come to mind, wrap them in bubbles. Allow them to float away and pop into nothing.

Elizabeth Onyeabor

Slip into this softening of your own heart. If you consider it a guilty pleasure, grant yourself this indulgence. Soak in the soothing, rising waters of self-compassion.

PRACTICE 9: PROPAGANDIZING PRATTLE

Now, we'll let your inner critic talk, but in a structured way.

I've adapted this practice from Thom Rutledge's book on self-forgiveness. (Rutledge 2012) It provides a tool to quiet critical self-talk.

Use two different colored pens, for example, blue and red. One color (blue) represents your positive thoughts and the other color (red) negative ones—your propagandizer.

1. *Create a positive list.*

   Focus on uplifting aspects of yourself. List what you see as your positive aspects, features, or qualities in blue. As soon as you jot down the first statement, you may notice an adverse reaction, the *but* part of the equation. For example, "I have a nice smile, *but* I don't floss enough, and my bottom teeth are crooked and . . ." Write the *but* parts using the red pen. Allow your inner critic to carry on this way until it chides no more about that aspect.

   Move on to another positive aspect, feature, or quality. Again, write the positive part in blue ink and the *but* (negative) part in red ink.

   Continue until you list between five to ten positive qualities along with your negative reactions to them.

2. *Create a negative list.*

   Create a new list but initially focus on what you see as your negative aspects, features, or traits. Write the negative part first with the red pen. After your propagandizer has had its say, your voice of reason should start the *but* part as something more positive. For example, "I'm not creative or artistic, *but* I have used creativity and artistry in the way I put words and ideas together for clients." Write the positive part in blue.

   Move on to another negative aspect, feature, or trait. Again, write the negative part in red ink and the *but* (positive) part in blue ink.

   Continue until you list between five to ten negative aspects along with your positive reactions to them.

   The more we suppress, the louder our critic wants to shout. Basically, it wants to be heard but it feels so hurtful we shut it out. This practice allows its expression and should quiet critique for a while. Return to this practice whenever your inner critic starts beating up on you.

PRACTICE 10: BLOSSOMING BRILLIANCE

TAKE DEEP BREATHS, and picture your beloved in your mind's eye. He or she may be who you chose for Practice 7 (Comforting Caress) or another companion you cherish.

1. *Bask in brilliance.*

   Focus on love pouring through your beloved. Visualize him or her showered with brilliant golden beams. He or she is glowing with love.

   Now, notice a white light radiating from your own body joining together with the gentle glow of your beloved. Bask in the brilliance for a moment.

2. *Describe the sensations.*

   Hold space for yourself while you write as fast as you can to express all the emotions the love and light infuses in you.

   When you've captured all the emotions of the experience, thank your beloved for sharing the light and rest for a few moments while your beloved's healing light penetrates through you.

3. *Note your beloved's comforting characteristics*

   Focus on your beloved's gentlest nature and describe all the traits you find most comforting. Jot down whatever words pop up until you can find no other words left to describe your beloved's admirable attributes.

Rest with those thoughts a few moments. Note the power of the words you've written.

4. *Reflect on your beloved's attributes.*

Now, gaze in a mirror, refer to the characteristics you noted, and say these words aloud:

"My beloved is full of [attribute]."

"That serves as a mirror for me. I am also full of [attribute]."

Do this until you've said all the words you listed in step three. Continue alternating each word first about your beloved and second about yourself.

In the exquisite, impassioned part of yourself, these praises about your beloved may well describe your blossoming brilliance. You likely see and most admire these aspects of your beloved because they represent aspects of yourself, even if you don't yet see them.

Allow the words to wrap you in a comforting cocoon. Before your change is complete, you may exert effort just as the butterfly does before it emerges and flies free. For now, relax within this chrysalis. Allow all the praises about your beloved to create a dawning perception of yourself.

You are, indeed, more exquisite than you realize.

PRACTICE 11:
INNER INSIGHTS

IN MY YOUTH, I rode on a mini roller coaster called the Wild Mouse. Unlike a traditional ride, its wooden track bent with unexpected twists and hairpin turns. The cart appeared to roll forward but jerked and veered to the left or right. One moment, I expected to speed downward, but instead, it clattered upward or vice versa.

Life lurches along like the Wild Mouse ride when we hinge our meaning and joy on other people and situations. They disappoint and deal unexpected jolts into our lives. Our own behavior can dissatisfy us, too, and may even surprise us.

Our wild ride can stop when we opt for a different path or another ride in life's amusement park. A clearer image forms through our practices.

Life's ups and downs don't go away. Instead, we choose our response. Have you ever been on a ride when your stomach flips in excitement as you hurtle up or down? Life can both thrill and terrify when traveling into uncharted territory.

1. *Locate your inner light.*

   Picture yourself in a place of natural beauty. Imagine the pleasant smells tickling your nose, joyful sounds resounding in your ears, and gentle air touching your skin.

Visualize another person approaching you. This person seems somehow familiar, but you cannot quite place him or her. A radiant light envelops him or her, like an angel. But you recognize this is a real person. This figure exudes enormous love. Even from a distance, the love embraces you fully. Wrapped within its comfort, you sense tremendous wisdom. At that moment, you recognize the shimmering person is an older, wiser *you*.

You delight at the idea and welcome the emerging wisdom. You also sense your more mature self offers wholeness, healing, and buoyancy.

Let's call this sage self your "Light Within."

2. *Listen to your Light Within.*

   As you soften into the calming tranquility, you hear your Light Within's voice. "Inhale and exhale three deep breaths so you can hear what I say. Clear away confusion from your mind. Watch your thoughts float upward in translucent word bubbles until they pop mid-air and evaporate into the atmosphere."

   Ask any questions you want about what needs to happen in your healing process or whatever you most desire answers for.

3. *Document your conversation.*

   Write down the answers you hear. Include both your reactions and resistance (if any) to what your Light Within tells you.

   When you've documented your conversation, thank your Light Within for the guidance and allow his or her radiance and wisdom to absorb into your body.

PRACTICE 12:
FINDING YOUR FRANCES

Several ancestors inspire my fire. Yours can, too. Your her-story or his-story and your ancestors' pasts may intertwine in ways you're not yet aware.

1. *Explore ancestors' stories.*

   If possible, read their stories about obstacles they endured and overcame. You may realize you possess the same ability, or perhaps a greater one, to solve challenges.

2. *Capture your experiences.*

   Your story is brilliant and touching. Imagine reading your her-story or his-story to your descendants, other family members, or friends as a fairy tale of sorts.

   Once upon a time, you lived in a beautiful and terrible world. You faced an almost insurmountable ordeal, but a prince charming or a fairy princess helped you conquer it. You lived happily ever after.

   The prince or princess wasn't another person but actually a power within yourself. The happily ever after part happened because of your efforts in overcoming the difficulty and maintaining your joy. Happiness and contentment radiated from within as you stoked a fiery passion and purpose. An inner fire burned bright once you found its never-ending fuel source.

Each person glows differently, so what feeds yours may vary from mine. However, your shimmer holds the same radiance. Nurture your Light Within. Coax the embers and spark the flames until brilliance guides your way.

You create both the light outshining your darkness and the darkness dowsing your light. You possess the power to flip the switch and focus on either one. It may not seem within your control, yet. Forge ahead one step at a time. It will become easier with practice.

You can find a smoother way when you name and face your troubles instead of smothering them. You can discover comfort within discomfort's mantle.

In Hamlet, Shakespeare's character, Polonius said, "to thine own self be true." (Shakespeare 1998) I encourage you to learn about your truest self and document your stories.

3. *Maintain compassionate self-exploration.*

Periodically continue to compassionately explore what bothers you about yourself.

It may no longer seem foreign and painful as you shift focus and channel your energy into exposing the distressing roots and uncover its partner, joy. They're conjoined opposites. Observe both.

You can discover and uncover a gift—the present you always held within yourself. Your reward is the ability to heal yourself. This is self-development's promise.

Search your heart and allow it to guide you through continuous self-exploration. Reconnect with your core and offer yourself compassion. Do this regularly to maintain healthy habits.

The Light Within

I close my eyes, seek the cuddle chair, and ask Mom's advice—any other encouragement for you to walk a brilliant, loving path. She reminds me of another treasure. The kindness, concern, and consideration coming from your beloved is the same compassion to offer yourself, especially when you judge yourself least worthy.

You hold something valuable to share. You are meant to accomplish something only *you* can do in this world. Not somebody else. *You.*

You, alone, define your worth and power.

Whether you believe it now or not, it can happen. As you practice and seek support from others who appreciate your self-development efforts, you will feel lighter. These may take time and practice.

Through healing habits, one day you'll realize you've given yourself an immense gift. Does that sound strange? Adversity offers a gift. The ordeal itself is not the gift. Your present is what you discover about yourself—meaning, passion, purpose, and self-love. Those are priceless, shining jewels. Nobody can take them from you. But they can fade without the regular practices that make love shine.

Let your Light Within shine with the compassion and love you deserve.

Remember, Frances means *a free one*. The key to your freedom lies within your reach.

Unlock the Frances inside you and fly on newfound wings.

REFERENCES

Covey, Stephen R. 2004. *7 Habits of Highly Effective People: Powerful Lessons in Personal Change.* New York: Free Press: A Division of Simon & Schuster.

DeLaMare, Mary Frances and Wills, Robert Donlon (transcribed by), 1935-1936. 1986. *The Life of Sophia Lois Flint Wills.* printed by Clayton, Lois Darlene Simmerman.

Epstein, Joseph. 2002. *Opinion: Think You Have a Book in You? Think Again.* September 28. https://www.nytimes.com/2002/09/28/opinion/think-you-have-a-book-in-you-think-again.html.

Howell, Kelly. 1999. *Guided Meditation: Stress Reduction Therapy.* Comp. Brain Sync.

Karpman, Dr. Stephen B. 2014. *A Game Free Life: The Definitive Book on the Drama Triangle and Compassion Triangle by the Originator and Author.* Drama Triangle Publications.

Onyeabor, Elizabeth. 2016. *From the Shadows: A Journey of Self-Discovery and Renewal.* Sojourn Publishing.

Rutledge, Thom. 2012. *The Power of Self-Forgiveness: Treating Yourself with the Love & Respect That You Might Not Know You Deserve.* New Harbinger Publications.

1998. *The Waterboy*. Directed by Frank Coraci. Produced by Touchstone Pictures. Performed by Adam Sandler, Kathy Bates, Fairuza Balk, Jerry Reed and Henry Winkler.

Schiller D, Monfils MH, Raio CM, Johnson DC, LeDoux JE, Phelps EA. 2009. "Preventing the return of fear in humans using reconsolidation update mechanisms." *Nature*.

Seligman, M.E.P. 1972. "Learned Helplessness." *Annual Review of Medicine*.

Shakespeare, William. 1998. *The Tragedy of Hamlet, Prince of Denmark*. ebook: Project Gutenberg.

Simmerman, Ruby Lois Wills, and Ernest M. edited by Simmerman. 1980. *The Robert Wills Family*.

Whitworth, Kathleen Pederson (transcribed by). 2004. *Mary DeLaMare Pederson: Excerpts from her Diaries and Letters 1933-1980*. (unpublished manuscript).

Whitworth, Kathleen Pederson. 2008. *Mary DeLaMare Pederson, Personal History*. (unpublished manuscript).

Whitworth, Kathleen Pederson. 1998. *Mary Frances Wills DeLaMare Life Sketches*.

Whitworth, Kathleen Pederson. 2010. *The Robert Guy DeLaMare Family: 1887-1990*.

Yensen, William. 2014. *Chakra Balancing & Healing Guided Meditation*. Comp. Frequency 21.

Zink, Sharon. 2017. *97% of Writers Never Finish their Novels: Here's Why*. May 23. http://sharonzink.com/writing-tips/97-of-writers-never-finish-their-novels-heres-why/.

ABOUT THE AUTHOR

Coach, poet, and award-winning, best-selling author Elizabeth Onyeabor loves sharing stories of hope and healing. Deeply drawn to expand self-love's light within us all, she founded the Habitual Happiness Hub. As Chief Ease of Excellence Officer, she coaches and inspires people around the world ready to embrace their whole selves, create lasting joy, and live their dreams.

Elizabeth is the proud mother of three grown children. A transplant from sunny Arizona, she now basks in the shimmering sub-Saharan sun with her beloved husband.

Read More

From the Shadows: A Journey of Self-Discovery and Renewal
Escaping the Shadows: A Pilgrimage with Poetry

Gifts

Access a practice guide, visualization recordings, and other gifts at www.ElizabethOnyeabor.com/gifts.

Work with Me

Book a discovery session with me. Let's explore your needs and how to live your dreams.
www.habitualhappinesshub.com/hhhcalendar

Connect with Me

ElizabethOnyeaborAuthor
elizabethonyeabor
efonyeabor

www.ingramcontent.com/pod-product-compliance
Lightning Source LLC
Chambersburg PA
CBHW021424070526

44577CB00001B/44